Budgeting for Higher Education at the State Level:
Enigma, Paradox, and Ritual

by Daniel T. Layzell and Jan W. Lyddon

ASHE-ERIC Higher Education Report 4, 1990

Prepared by

Clearinghouse on Higher Education
The George Washington University

In cooperation with

Association for the Study
of Higher Education

Published by

School of Education and Human Development
The George Washington University

Jonathan D. Fife, Series Editor

Cite as
Layzell, Daniel T., and Jan W. Lyddon. 1990. *Budgeting for Higher Education at the State Level: Enigma, Paradox, and Ritual.* ASHE-ERIC Higher Education Report No. 4. Washington, D.C.: The George Washington University, School of Education and Human Development.

Library of Congress Catalog Card Number 90-63845
ISSN 0884-0040
ISBN 1-878380-01-X

Managing Editor: Bryan Hollister
Manuscript Editor: Barbara Fishel/Editech
Cover design by Michael David Brown, Rockville, Maryland

The ERIC Clearinghouse on Higher Education invites individuals to submit proposals for writing monographs for the *ASHE-ERIC Higher Education Report* series. Proposals must include:
1. A detailed manuscript proposal of not more than five pages.
2. A chapter-by-chapter outline.
3. A 75-word summary to be used by several review committees for the initial screening and rating of each proposal.
4. A vita and a writing sample.

ERIC Clearinghouse on Higher Education
School of Education and Human Development
The George Washington University
One Dupont Circle, Suite 630
Washington, DC 20036-1183

This publication was prepared partially with funding from the Office of Educational Research and Improvement, U.S. Department of Education, under contract no. ED RI-88-062014. The opinions expressed in this report do not necessarily reflect the positions or policies of OERI or the Department.

EXECUTIVE SUMMARY

State budgeting for higher education is a complex set of activities involving various competing interests and issues. In the broadest sense, the primary objective of all budgeting is to target resources to meet specific policy objectives. The budget spans the distance between present choices and future options (Caiden 1988). While the federal government provides substantial support to higher education in the form of student aid and research grants, state governments bear the principal responsibility in budgeting for higher education operations and thus in shaping the present and future direction of higher education within the state.

The simplicity of this description belies the underlying interplay of human and external forces and factors laced throughout the budget process. Higher education is both similar to and different from other policy areas in state government like transportation or corrections. It is similar in that it must compete with these other areas for its share of a sometimes shrinking budget. It is different in that higher education is relatively autonomous from the state.

What Are the Environmental Factors Framing the State Budget Process for Higher Education?

The environmental context is comprised of interrelated historical, political, economic, and demographic factors. Historical factors include state residents' traditional values and preferences regarding higher education as well as the state government's historical involvement in governance of higher education. Previous budgets also make up part of the historical context. Political factors include the structure of higher education, gubernatorial influence, legislative influence, and interest groups' and citizens' influences. Economic factors include a state's general economic condition, state tax capacity, and availability of state revenues. Demographic factors include the level and composition of a state's population, enrollment in higher education, and student participation rates in higher education.

How Do These Factors Affect State Budgeting for Higher Education?

In part, these factors help explain the wide variance in funding for higher education among the states, although by no means do they explain all of the variance. A state's historical traditions act as "behavioral regulators" for the participants in the state budget process. If the state's residents traditionally have highly valued higher education, state policy makers will also generally value it, and vice versa. Political factors determine the extent to which the power of higher education is centralized at the state level (that is, coordinating agency) or diffused among the individual institutions and the predominance of the governor and the legislature in the budget process. In recent years, governors generally have become much more deeply involved in higher education and hence the budget process. Legislators have also become increasingly sophisticated in their understanding of higher education policy. Consequently, as states' involvement in higher education has increased, so have fears of diminished autonomy within the academy.

State support for higher education is directly related to the general condition of a state's economy, state tax capacity, and availability of revenues. If a state's economy is faltering, then its capacity to raise revenues and thus the level of revenues available are diminished substantially. Further, as state economies worsen, demands on the state budget from other services, such as public aid and corrections, also increase. Demographic forces, such as the aging of the population and the growth of the number of minority students, will affect state budgeting for higher education as state governments strive to meet the special needs of these individuals. Traditionally, enrollments and higher education participation rates have been important factors in determining the level of funding provided to higher education, but some evidence suggests that the significance of these factors may be decreasing.

What Are the Primary Elements of the State Budget Process for Higher Education?

The elements of the state budget process for higher education include the participants, timing, and strategies to allocate resources. The major actors in the process are the governor, the legislature, their staffs, and the higher education community. Both governors and legislatures are asserting themselves more strongly in this process, albeit for different reasons, as a result of increasing sophistication, concern about higher education's outcomes, and recognition of the economic importance of higher education. The governor must represent the broad spectrum of state needs, while legislators are more concerned with specific needs of constituents or regions. The higher education community is comprised of the state-level coordinating or governing agency (if any) and the various sectors of higher education, both public and private.

As important as the governor, legislature, and the higher education governing and coordinating boards are the staffs of these entities. Almost two decades ago, these individuals were the "anonymous leaders of higher education" (Glenny 1972). If anything, it is even more true today. Staffs handle technical details, distinguish the important from the trivial, and generally serve as gatekeepers in the budget process.

The timing of the budget process presents numerous issues as well. Over time, most states have shifted from biennial budgeting to annual budgeting to annual budgeting with mid-year alterations. Legislatures meet with greater frequency, economic conditions are shifting rapidly, and demands for state dollars have increased in number and intensity. Even states that still have biennial budgets meet midterm to make alterations. These changes have altered the utility of long-term planning for higher education. Further, participants in the state higher education budget process have different perspectives of the time frame. Politicians generally focus on short time frames, while the higher education community has a longer time frame for meeting objectives. Tensions arise when politicians want quick solutions to problems that require long-term commitments.

Techniques for allocating resources for higher education vary within and among states. Several states use a funding formula for some or all of the higher education budget. The effectiveness of funding formulas in meeting objectives for funding is essentially unknown. Almost half of the states use peer groups comprised of similar states and/or institutions for making decisions and justifying the budget for funding libraries, faculty salaries, staffing levels, and so on. Some states approach the funding of higher education from a more programmatic basis.

How Does the State Higher Education Budget Link Resources with State Objectives for Higher Education Policy?

The state higher education budget sets forth the state's major policy preferences for higher education. Major policy concerns in higher education in recent years have been accountability, costs, productivity, quality, affordability, economic development, access for minority and nontraditional students, and equity for independent higher education.

Accountability. Over time, the focus of accountability has evolved from a fiduciary orientation to one focused on outcomes. As a result, accountability mechanisms have begun to evolve from data-collection instruments to instruments of change. Future accountability mechanisms will likely be integrated into the state budget process to emphasize feedback.

Costs, productivity, and quality. These concepts are seen as inextricably linked. Costs of higher education are increasing rapidly as a result of a number of factors, including the lack of internal constraints on resources and the propensity of colleges and universities to grow rather than reallocate to meet needs. At the same time, little agreement on measures of outcomes leaves state policy makers concerned about productivity, or the lack of it, in higher education. Even more troublesome has been the goal of maintaining quality in higher education. In an effort to enhance quality, several states have devised incentive funding programs in areas such as undergraduate education and research. It remains clear, however, that the key to keeping costs down and productivity up, while maintaining quality in higher education, lies in the ability to formulate specific goals, exercise constraints on resources, and encourage innovation.

Affordability. As tuition outpaced general price inflation during the 1980s, the affordability of higher education took on greater significance. Some states have attempted to address this issue by linking tuition to external factors, such as price indices, serving to minimize the traditionally inverse relationship between tuition at public institutions and state appropriations for higher education. A second policy lever has been funding state student financial aid programs. States that have high tuition usually have well-funded student aid programs. A more recent development has been the advent of state programs for tuition prepayment and savings, although the effectiveness of these programs in addressing affordability is questionable. Evidence suggests that few states closely link policies for student aid, tuition, and institutional support, which would indicate a great deal of inefficiency in states' financing of higher education.

Economic development. States have also begun to involve higher education in economic development. State-funded economic development includes research programs, involvement in education and training programs for the work force, and fostering partnerships with business for the purpose of technology transfer. The effectiveness of these activities remains unclear. Numerous potential problems exist, including the highly political nature of economic development and the fundamental differences between higher education and business.

Minority and nontraditional students. Minority and nontraditional students present special concerns for state policy makers. Although minorities have increased as a percentage of the population, they have generally declined as a percentage of enrollments in higher education. Most states have initiated programs designed to increase minority students' retention and achievement, and some have been effective.

Nontraditional students are becoming the new majority in higher education, but neither state policy makers nor those in the higher education community have done much to change the structure of higher education to meet these students' special needs.

Independent higher education. State policy makers realize the important tangible and intangible benefits independent higher education provides to the states. As a result, many states provide financial support to the independent sector in the higher education budget through student aid and direct institutional aid programs. Because the independent sector highly values these programs, they are an important policy lever for the state.

What Do We Know about State-level Budgeting for Higher Education and What Are the Implications?
Budgeting for higher education is complex and multifaceted. As states become even more involved with higher education, the budget process will become even more important in initiating new policies and policy changes. At the same time, the analysis of the literature indicates several areas requiring

further research. For example, it is necessary to know more about the cultural and political context of budgeting for higher education. The effectiveness of higher education policies initiated through the budget process must be evaluated, including incentive funding for quality and economic development. The implications are twofold. First, it is evident that all participants in the state budget process for higher education would be well served to view the process in the "big picture." Understanding why certain things happen in the budget process can greatly improve participants' effectiveness in achieving objectives. Second and simply, state budgeting for higher education is an area ripe for research.

ADVISORY BOARD

CONSULTING EDITORS

Brenda M. Albright
State of Tennessee Higher Education Commission

Walter R. Allen
University of California

Leonard L. Baird
University of Kentucky

James H. Banning
Colorado State University

Trudy W. Banta
University of Tennessee

Margaret J. Barr
Texas Christian University

Louis W. Bender
Florida State University

Rita Bornstein
University of Miami

Larry Braskamp
University of Illinois

Pault T. Brinkman
National Center for Higher Education Management Systems

L. Leon Campbell
University of Delaware

Robert F. Carbone
University of Maryland

Susan Cohen
Lesley College

John W. Creswell
University of Nebraska

Mary E. Dilworth
ERIC Clearinghouse on Teacher Education

James A. Eison
Southeast Missouri State University

Valerie French
American University

Milton Greenberg
American University

Judith Dozier Hackman
Yale University

Brian L. Hawkins
Brown University

Edward R. Hines
Illinois State University

Joseph V. Julian
Syracuse University

Oscar T. Lenning
Robert Wesleyan College

Jeanne M. Likens
Ohio State University

Dierdre A. Ling
University of Massachusetts

James W. Lyons
Stanford University

Judith B. McLaughlin
Harvard University

Sherry Magill
Washington College

Andrew T. Masland
Digital Equipment Corporation

Yolanda T. Moses
California State University

Bernard Murchland
Ohio Wesleyan University

Michael T. Nettles
University of Tennessee

C. Gail Norris
Utah System of Education State Board of Regents

Elizabeth M. Nuss
National Association of Student Personnel Administrators

Edward H. O'Neil
Duke University

Robert L. Payton
Indiana University

Joseph F. Phelan
University of New Hampshire

James J. Rhatigan
Wichita State University

Steven K. Schultz
Westmont College

Mary Ellen Sheridan
Ohio State University

Robert L. Sizmon
Wake Medical Center

Charles U. Smith
Florida Agricultural and Mechanical University

Betty Taylor
Lesley College

Reginald Wilson
American Council on Education

REVIEW PANEL

Charles Adams
University of Amherst

Richard Alfred
University of Michigan

Philip G. Altbach
State University of New York

Louis C. Attinasi, Jr.
University of Houston

Ann E. Austin
Vanderbilt University

Robert J. Barak
State Board of Regents

Alan Bayer
Virginia Polytechnic Institute and State University

John P. Bean
Indiana University

Louis W. Bender
Florida State University

Carol Bland
University of Minnesota

Deane G. Bornheimer
New York University

John A. Centra
Syracuse University

Arthur W. Chickering
George Mason University

Jay L. Chronister
University of Virginia

Mary Jo Clark
San Juan Community College

Shirley M. Clark
University of Minnesota

Darrel A. Clowes
Virginia Polytechnic Institute and State University

CONTENTS

FOREWORD

In order to win, a contender must be able to play the game better than the competition. This is as true in sports and business as it is when competing for funds in the budgeting arena. There is another saying that applies when discussing budgeting: "You've got to know the system to beat the system." To know the budgeting system in higher education, one must understand the process of developing a budget, learn the rules governing successful budget-making, and recognize the key people involved.

On the surface, an organization's budget is a rational allocation of resources. On closer examination, a budget turns out to be a political document that reflects the values, vision, mission and purpose of an organization. Deeper still, that political document represents the sum of decisions made by many people with often widely divergent views.

The budget for a state higher education system represents the system's importance in the eyes of the state legislature and governor relative to the other programs vying for state funding. The budget for an individual institution reflects its importance vis-à-vis the other institutions in the system. The success of an institution in altering or controlling the direction of its budget essentially depends upon its ability to convince decision makers of its own importance within the historical, political, economic and demographic constraints of a state.

In this report, authors Daniel T. Layzell, higher education research analyst for the Arizona Joint Legislative Budget Committee, and Jan W. Lyddon, director of institutional research for Saginaw Valley State University, examine the entire process of state budgeting for higher education. From a conceptual overview and exploration of the environmental contexts of budgeting, to a final analysis and discussion of the report's implications, the authors provide an important body of knowledge for both researchers and practitioners.

It is important to understand that everyone in a leadership position who is affected by the institutional budget should make it their business to know how the budget is developed, and what part they may play in its design. The greater the understanding of budget development throughout an institution, the greater the ability of the organization to develop persuasive policies that can alter or protect a budget. Even if primary budget decisions are made centrally, it is important for the leadership of an institution to win institution-wide support for these decisions. This report by Layzell and Lyddon will do much to further such a broad understanding of the budget process.

Jonathan D. Fife
Series Editor
Professor of Higher Education and
Director, ERIC Clearinghouse on Higher Education
The George Washington University

INTRODUCTION

Winston Churchill once described Russia as a riddle wrapped in a mystery inside an enigma. To many in higher education, the state budget process is their Russia. Department heads at colleges and universities submit their budget requests for the next fiscal year and nine months later or so find out how much they will have to spend. This amount is almost always less than what they requested—sometimes substantially so. In between submission and allocation, this request becomes aggregated with the rest of the state higher education budget request for the next fiscal year, and seemingly contradictory events take place for not always clear reasons. By the time individuals at the department level receive their allocations, it is time to begin the process all over again, which in turn lends a ritualistic feeling to this annual or biennial confusion.

Is it a tail or a trunk or something completely different?

The objective of this monograph is to analyze state budgeting for the annual appropriations to higher education cohesively and comprehensively, in the process clarifying this important activity. States provide substantial funding to both public and private sectors of higher education. Funding for public higher education is primarily for general operating expenditures, both recurring and new. Funding for private higher education usually takes the form of student aid programs or, in some states, general and categorical grant programs for private institutions.

Many in higher education suffer from myopia when it comes to the budget process: They see only the parts that directly affect them. For many, the state higher education budget process is analogous to the old parable in which a group of blind men attempt to describe to one another what an elephant looks like. Is it a tail or a trunk or something completely different? This reaction is natural, given the complexity of this topic. This monograph attempts to treat separately the issues of context, procedure, and product or outcome within state budgeting for higher education. At the same time, however, it must be remembered that this process overlaps in several ways and has many links.

The literature synthesized in this monograph comes from both within and without the field of higher education. Much has been written on the budget process in general in other fields, such as political science, public administration, and economics. The literature analyzed in this monograph is predominantly from the 1980s, given the desire to use the most current literature base possible. A few references are made to earlier "classic" studies, however, and some areas of the budgeting process have no recent literature (see, e.g., Caruthers and Orwig 1979; Easton 1957; Fabricant 1952; Wirt and Kurst 1972). In addition, an effort has been made to include nontraditional references, such as policy studies by state coordinating agencies, to provide concrete examples of what has been occurring at the state level of budgeting for higher education. At the outset of this project, the authors contacted state higher education finance officers (SHEFOs) from several states and asked them to provide any recent (since 1980) studies or other materials relevant to higher education budgeting in their states. All were infinitely helpful in their responses and suggestions.

For many states, the 1980s were a watershed with regard to funding higher education. As table 1 shows, several states had large increases in state tax support for higher education during the 1980s. Massachusetts is one such example, although as the "miracle" diminished in the last part of the decade, so too did state support. Conversely, states that had historically provided significant support to higher education (Illinois, Michigan, and Pennsylvania, for example) lagged behind the rest in the 1980s. The reason for this variance is a mixture of economics, demographics, and politics. Regardless of whether a state provided substantial or little increase in funding for higher education during the 1980s, this topic has become increasingly important to all states as they struggle to resolve the policy issues currently facing higher education.

TABLE 1

APPROPRIATIONS OF STATE TAX FUNDS FOR HIGHER EDUCATION OPERATING EXPENSES: FISCAL YEARS 1980, 1988, AND 1990
($000)

	1980	1988	1990	Percent Change 1988 to 1990	Percent Change 1980 to 1990
Maine	$57,336	$141,412	$176,868	25.1%	208.5%
Massachusetts	314,929	894,998	815,998	(8.8)	159.1
Nevada	56,896	112,551	146,636	30.3	157.7
Washington	310,133	673,972	790,383	17.3	154.9
Maryland	323,732	614,605	823,348	34.0	154.3
North Carolina	580,190	1,284,076	1,458,516	13.6	151.4
New Hampshire	29,806	66,901	74,393	11.2	149.6

TABLE 1 (continued)

APPROPRIATIONS OF STATE TAX FUNDS FOR HIGHER EDUCATION OPERATING EXPENSES

	1980	1988	1990	Percent Change 1988 to 1990	Percent Change 1980 to 1990
Virginia	444,054	915,836	1,107,480	20.9%	149.4%
Arizona	232,707	498,036	569,982	14.4	144.9
Florida	650,334	1,367,174	1,567,712	14.7	141.1
New Jersey	477,891	1,016,773	1,142,805	12.4	139.1
Hawaii	124,359	243,118	292,456	20.3	135.2
Georgia	385,132	759,404	884,669	16.5	129.7
North Dakota	61,822	115,723	139,911	20.9	126.3
Alabama	344,683	669,992	776,641	15.9	125.3
Wyoming	51,664	111,583	116,183	4.1	124.9
Vermont	27,062	49,990	59,936	19.9	121.5
Delaware	53,273	101,339	115,541	14.0	116.9
Tennessee	335,612	636,322	727,449	14.3	116.8
New Mexico	138,624	262,813	296,410	12.8	113.8
Ohio	669,197	1,265,213	1,427,041	12.8	113.2
New York	1,543,416	2,874,893	3,185,045	10.8	106.4
Connecticut	226,371	414,174	463,796	12.0	104.9
Colorado	246,866	441,070	504,757	14.4	104.5
Indiana	398,997	704,703	814,021	15.5	104.0
California	2,814,321	5,071,271	5,740,737	13.2	104.0
Rhode Island	71,725	127,759	144,522	13.1	101.5
Texas	1,315,525	2,231,785	2,624,288	17.6	99.5
Minnesota	477,731	815,663	946,779	16.1	98.2
Oklahoma	228,827	394,404	453,090	14.9	98.0
Utah	138,787	257,218	272,201	5.8	96.1
Nebraska	150,940	227,974	290,491	27.4	92.5
Missouri	314,807	503,019	603,535	20.0	91.7
South Carolina	320,412	521,016	612,508	17.6	91.2
Kansas	238,839	361,178	444,788	23.1	86.2
Idaho	85,028	139,136	158,247	13.7	86.1
Mississippi	233,834	360,036	432,971	20.3	85.2
Alaska	95,906	165,542	176,023	6.3	83.5
Kentucky	299,918	494,949	550,182	11.2	83.4
Pennsylvania	742,415	1,173,572	1,361,361	16.0	83.4
Montana	60,494	105,106	109,416	4.1	80.9
Illinois	931,489	1,331,777	1,675,322	25.8	79.9
Iowa	282,114	441,458	502,293	13.8	78.0
Arkansas	169,664	284,333	301,200	5.9	77.5
Michigan	808,320	1,303,202	1,408,009	8.0	74.2

TABLE 1 (continued)

APPROPRIATIONS OF STATE TAX FUNDS FOR HIGHER EDUCATION OPERATING EXPENSES

	1980	1988	1990	Percent Change 1988 to 1990	Percent Change 1980 to 1990
Oregon	$229,013	$349,940	$395,898	13.1%	72.9%
Wisconsin	468,618	705,430	784,141	11.2	67.3
South Dakota	52,251	73,732	85,995	16.6	64.6
West Virginia	158,119	237,404	251,505	5.9	59.1
Louisiana	330,008	494,507	522,912	5.7	58.5
Total	**$19,104,191**	**$34,408,082**	**$39,326,391**	**14.3%**	**105.9%**

Source: Grapevine, October/November 1989, No. 358, p. 2262.

A CONCEPTUAL OVERVIEW OF STATE BUDGETING

Once people looked to the stars to tell what the future would bring; today they look at the budget. The budget spans the distance between present choices and future options (Caiden 1988). While the federal government provides substantial support to higher education in the form of student aid and research grants, state governments bear the principal responsibility for budgeting for public higher education operations. Thus, state governments are the principal participants in shaping both the present and the future of higher education.

A basic framework is the starting point for understanding state budgeting. The framework cannot depict the details, but it provides a basis for understanding the major conditions, players, responses, and outcomes of state budgeting. Such a framework includes environmental factors, the state organizational filter, a funding approach, and outcomes of dollars appropriated and goals achieved and evaluated (see figure 1). Each state has its own conditions, both environmental and within the government, just as each state's appropriations outcome is distinctive.

FIGURE 1

STATE BUDGETING FOR HIGHER EDUCATION: A CONCEPTUAL FRAMEWORK

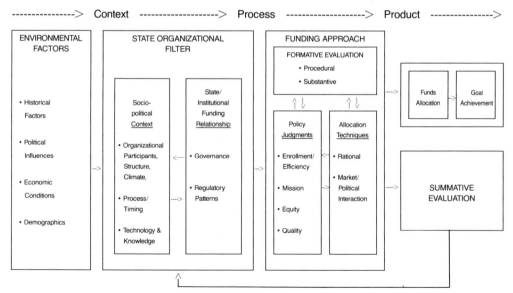

Source: Lyddon, Fonte, and Miller 1986.

Although the elements are disaggregated for the purpose of analysis, it should be stressed that much overlap occurs within the state budget process for higher education. The following sections loosely group these conceptual elements under the descriptors "context," "process," and "product."

Environmental Factors

Conditions outside both state government and higher education can affect state budgeting. This subsection outlines these conditions and how they relate to budget outcomes; the next section discusses changes occurring in the conditions themselves. Precisely how these conditions affect budgetary outcomes and processes has been the subject of numerous studies, beginning with Solomon Fabricant in 1952. Fabricant, Ira Sharkansky, Thomas Dye, and others conducted studies of state budgeting behaviors and outcomes. The environment includes conditions that are generally recognized as external to the current relationship between the state and higher education as well as conditions of the past funding relationship between them. An example of the latter is previous state budgets for higher education. They are included in environmental conditions because they exert influence on the current state–higher education relationship, just as economic, political, and demographic conditions influence the relationship. Four categories of environmental conditions typically are included in these studies: (1) historical factors, (2) political factors, (3) economic factors, and (4) demographic factors.

Historical factors and budget outcomes

Historical factors include past state budgeting practices and higher education's past share of the state's budget that tangibly affect budget outcomes as well as less tangible historical factors, such as state culture and traditions. Most of the past literature has focused on the more tangible historical factors, such as incrementalism. Although scant evidence exists, it could be that historical factors, such as the organizational cultures of state government and higher education institutions, significantly affect the budget outcome for higher education as well.

The first proposition about budgeting today is that "last year's allocation is the absolute minimum to be expected from the state this year" (D. Jones 1984, p. 64). The inviolability of the base is frequently referred to as "incrementalism," that is, the gradual progression building upon previous decisions (see, e.g., Wildavsky 1984). Incrementalism—or limited, non-comprehensive change—was the most common method of budgeting at one time. "If anything can be said about the differences in incremental budgeting at state and federal levels, it is that state personnel seem to be even more fascinated with the dollar-increment of change in an agency's budget proposal" (Sharkansky 1970, p. 56). Another researcher found that, in three midwestern states' spending on higher education, the previous appropriation was the single greatest predictor of states' spending on higher education (Lingenfelter 1974).

Despite many studies that have shown the importance of the previous appropriation in predicting subsequent appropriations, however, the concept of incrementalism in budgeting has been challenged. Wildavsky's study of the federal government noted that its budgets experienced "shift points" during the period 1947 to 1963. This measurement of non-stable incremental behavior appears to be unique in the literature on government budgeting, and Wildavsky suggests several reasons for the existence of shift points: accounting, congressional supervision, reorganization of activities from one agency to another, external variables, new laws, changes in appropriations policies, partisan controversies, or unidentified issues (Wildavsky 1986). Further, while state spending for higher education was largely incremental, it did not progress forward in steady, predictable jumps (Lyddon 1989). A study of the 50 states showed that each state's regression line had breaks occurring at different points in the 25-year period (1960 to 1985). And incrementalism has been criticized as a theory of budgeting that provides "an irresistible description of the budgetary process" (LeLoup 1988, p. 35). Budgeting has changed in recent years from a process that is primarily concerned with bottom-up and line-item decisions (microbudgeting) to a process focused on high-level decisions on spending, relative budget shares, and a top-down approach (macrobudgeting). Although the latter study was conducted on the federal budget, not on state budgets, experience in Michigan and Illinois indicates that some evidence of macrobudgeting is occurring in state appropriations. Slower growth in revenues, increased competition between political parties, and efforts to shift existing funds into more politically popular program areas have occurred (LeLoup 1988).

In making budgetary decisions, state governments must deal with many competing areas. The needs of education, welfare, public health, and other state-sponsored services often conflict, and spending for one area may mean a trade-off against spending for another area. In Tennessee, for example, the governor promised to increase starting salaries for teachers in elementary and secondary schools—which could cause a ripple effect if higher education and state employees push for similar salary increases (National Conference 1988).

In essence, most of the literature on historical factors and state budgeting has dealt with concrete factors, such as the share of the budget and incrementalism. Some observers have suggested, however, that less quantifiable historical factors like political culture and traditions also significantly affect the outcome of the state budget for higher education (see, e.g., Fisher 1988a; Garms 1986).

Political variables and budget outcomes

Changes in political factors also appear to have relatively little influence on changes in states' *total spending*. Changes in party strength, however, were consistently related to changes in the *amount and proportion* spent on education and other specific budgetary categories in states with four-year gubernatorial terms (Jones 1974). Higher education is political in the same sense that other entities of state government are political. Universities and colleges are subject to demands from the environment, as are all other government systems. And higher education is political because the institutions have links with the formal authority of the state political system (Wirt 1976).

Little recent literature addresses the effect of political factors on funding outcomes, for much of the research was conducted in the 1960s and early 1970s. Those researchers found in general, however, that the statistically measurable relationship between political or governmental variables and policy outcomes was very low. Political variables are not predictor variables. They do not have direct effects but are reflections of socioeconomic characteristics of the states in which they exhibit their effects (Dawson and Robinson 1963; Sharkansky and Hofferbert 1969).

The lack of direct communication between members of the public and state politicians regarding higher education creates difficulty in tracing cause and effect in educational policy making (Eulau 1971). The exchange that occurs is "sporadic and unorganized, usually dealing with some specific matter but not with higher education as an institutional concern of society" (p. 213). This observation is still true in that citizens' contacts about higher education usually have more to do with tuition, financial aid, or admission policies at particular institutions. Rarely do citizens write or call a politician with a concern about the entire higher education system or about overall state financing of higher education or about much beyond their individual interests. Nevertheless, in recent years it appears that higher education as a political issue has increased in salience for politicians, and higher education as an interest group has increased greatly in importance. The advent of incentive programs, the increase in overall spending beyond the rate of inflation, and other outcomes indicate some form of political demand.

Economic variables and budget outcomes

Economic variables have direct relationships with state appropriations. Wealth is one economic variable that is important because it is an expression of a state's ability to pay for services. Frequently used indicators of wealth are personal income and availability of general revenues. The earliest such study found that per capita income within a state was the main determinant of the level of the state government's expenditures (Fabricant 1952). Later studies using per capita personal income have shown mixed results with respect to the prediction of total state spending for higher education; the principal difference occurs with what outcome is being predicted. For example, two studies in the mid-1970s showed that per capita income had no significant effect on state higher education expenditures per capita (Lingenfelter 1974; Peterson 1973), but the same two studies showed that per capita income did have a highly significant effect on overall *percentage* increases in public expenditures for higher education. A recent study also found a significant positive relationship between personal income per capita and state higher education expenditures per capita (Garms 1986), while another found that per capita income within a state had no significant effect on state aid per student at major research institutions (Coughlin and Erekson 1986). Clearly, the influence of per capita income on state appropriations for higher education deserves further study.

In most cases, the availability of general revenues has been found to be very closely associated with state spending for higher education (Coughlin and Erekson 1986; Garms 1986).

Demographic variables and budget outcomes

Demographic variables in many studies have been used to modify an economic variable, usually to permit comparisons among states. For example, a study might examine state appropriations per student enrolled or the effect of per capita income on budget outcomes. At other times, demographic variables have been used as individual variables together with economic or political variables.

The specific results of studies of relationships between demographic variables and budget outcomes are not clearly summarized. Of the four categories of variables, demographic variables have been treated least consistently in the literature, although the most often tested demographic variable is some form of college enrollments. Enrollment has been measured in a variety of ways—full-time equivalent (FTE) students, head counts, FTE students enrolled as a percentage of the college-age population, or change in enrollment over time. Statistically, the relationships between state spending for higher education and measures of enrollment have included correlations, time series and trend analyses, and multiple regression.

Enrollment is included as part of environmental conditions, although one might consider it internal. Some justification exists for including it here. For one thing, enrollment is a preexisting condition. Funding formulas can depend, at least in part, on the number of students enrolled in previous years as a basis for funding considerations. For another, enrollment is not exclusively the domain of the state. Decisions regarding admissions, including the number and mix of students, are generally the institution's domain.

The results of studies attempting to link enrollment with state appropriations have been contradictory. One study noted "a strong correlation between college costs to the states and enrollment" (Kim and Price 1977, p. 256). In contrast, another found very weak relationships between changes in enrollment and changes in revenue in California (Jones 1978). A study of state appropriations to higher education between 1968 and 1977 found that the change in spending was independent of changes in enrollments in higher education (Ruyle and Glenny 1979). And another more recent study found that increased enrollments in public institutions typically resulted in a net loss of state appropriations per FTE student (Leslie and Ramey 1986). These contradictory results may be the result of many factors, including the inherent distinctiveness of each state's budgeting process.

The State Organizational Filter
The state organizational filter is the first portion of the state's response to the external environment. It has two major components: the broad sociopolitical context and the more specific relationships between the state and its higher education community. Each state filters its environmental conditions in certain ways. A state may respond to one set of environmental conditions but not another, or it may respond quickly to a third condition and more slowly to a fourth. One set of actors in the process might respond, while others do not respond at all to certain conditions. For example, one state's tax structure may be based largely on sales taxes (Florida, for example), which could mean that because the yield from an income tax varies more over the business cycle than the yield of a general sales tax, a state with an income tax system may react more quickly to economic changes than one with a revenue system based on a sales tax (Mikesell 1984).

The state organizational filter, however, further modifies the impact of those environmental changes on the state's higher education system. For example, a state with declining revenues might treat higher education the same as all other state-funded activities, while in another state, higher education might be somewhat protected (or conversely unprotected) from falling revenues because of factors in the state organizational filter. In 1985, for example, the Texas Legislative Budget Board, facing falling revenue from oil and gas, recommended drastic cuts in higher education but no cuts in other state agencies. "The board could have gone back and reduced its recommended appropriations for all state agencies, but it did not. The easy, quick way . . . was to pull it all out of higher [education], . . . [which] is exactly what the board did. Thus the recommendation for a 26 percent decrease" (Biemiller 1985, p. 13).

The relationship between the state and institutional funding goes even farther in modifying responses to environmental conditions. Again, using the example of Texas, the University of Texas system had been established so that it would have

. . . the University of Texas System had been established so that it would have a power base in the political system.

a power base in the political system. The formal governance relationship was developed to ensure that the system had institutions in each region of the state so it could cover legislative votes (Biemiller 1985). The inclusion or creation of institutions on the basis of a relationship with legislators, a governor, or other powerful interests is, as shown in Texas in 1985, a means of modifying the state's responses to environmental conditions. The University of Texas system relied on its political clout from every region of the state to avert the proposed 26 percent cut in its budget.

Sociopolitical context

The principal components of the sociopolitical context are (1) organizational participants, structure, and climate; (2) process issues, including timing; and (3) technology and knowledge bases of the state. While each state is different, they exhibit some commonalities. For example, each state has similar types of decision makers in the budgeting process, though they have different formal and informal roles and different levels of impact on the outcome. Every state has a governor, a legislature, and some sort of statewide coordinating or governing body for higher education, with the exception of Wyoming, which has no designated statewide postsecondary body (McGuinness 1988).

Organizational participants in state budgeting. The governor generally serves as a state's chief budget officer. In that role, he or she generally sets the overall tone and parameters of the budget, consolidates budget requests from agencies, lobbies the legislature on budget items, approves or vetoes the budget, and implements and controls the budget (Adler and Lane 1988). The ability to exert leadership on public policy, whether in the budget or other areas of policy, depends on a variety of factors and the fit among those factors:

1. *The condition and tradition of a state at any point...*
2. *The perceived need for action in higher education made up of policy issues and political demands coming from higher education*
3. *The governor as an individual*
4. *The formal powers of the governor*
5. *The governor's ability to influence policy making, especially to build networks with other participants in the*

*policy-making process and to establish a policy agenda
for state government* (Adler and Lane 1988, p. 8).

The state budget office, a part of the executive branch, is
also an important participant in the process. Its formal and
informal roles differ from state to state as well as within states
over time. The orientations of state budget offices toward their
roles "reflect differences in tradition, views of appropriate institutional relationships, perspectives on how best to serve
the governor, and patterns of job expectation and staff recruitment. While states may differ on these 'givens,' [it] does not
suggest that a budget director and staff are more or less in-
fluential within their own state than are others within their
respective states" (Gosling 1987, p. 63). Little attention is
given in the literature to the roles and influence of state budget offices in policy making as opposed to budgeting.

In contrast to governors' roles in setting agendas, legislatures more typically see their roles as parochial and directed
more at assisting constituents. Thus, the legislature tends to
operate more narrowly on distributive and redistributive matters (Brandl 1988). Like the research about state budget offices, research on state legislatures and their policy making
is limited, partly because of the difficulty of building gener-
alizations on 50 diverse settings (Oppenheimer 1985). One
important factor is the increasing number and professionalism
of legislative staffs (Davis 1984) and their impact on the process. The staff is crucial in reducing the reliance of legislators
on lobbyists (BeVier 1979).

Process and timing. Budgeting is geared to a cycle that allows a state to absorb and respond to new information. The
cycle has four phases, each with its own primary actors and
its own time line: preparation and submission, approval, execution, and audit. Several phases, affecting different budget
years, could be occurring at any given time. The entire period
in which each phase occurs can vary greatly from a few weeks
to many months (Lee and Johnson 1983).

Responsibility for preparation and submission of the state
budget varies greatly, though at the state level, it usually falls
to the governor and the budget office to coordinate the effort.
In some states, such as Mississippi, the responsibility for preparing the budget falls to a legislative commission (Lee and
Johnson 1983). In some instances, the higher education coor-

dinating or governing body also plays a role in preparing and submitting budgets.

Budget approval is nearly always a function of the legislature. Some states place all state budget areas within a single appropriations bill, while others have as many as hundreds of appropriations bills. A legislature might be legally restricted in the degree of change it can make in the governor's budget; for example, the Maryland and Nebraska legislatures are restricted in their ability to increase the budget. The last step of the approval process is signing the appropriation into law—or vetoing all or part of it. In no case can a governor augment the budget beyond what is provided by the legislature (Lee and Johnson 1983).

Execution is the third phase, and it begins with the fiscal year. It is common to have some form of centralized control during this phase, such as a state controller's or treasurer's office. Such control includes apportioning the fiscal year's funds in some manner throughout the year to ensure that agencies do not spend all their available funds in less than the fiscal year and that agencies do not transfer large amounts between budget lines (Lee and Johnson 1983).

The final phase is the audit, the original purpose of which was to guarantee executive compliance with the provisions of appropriations bills. The scope of auditing has been broadened in recent years to include assessments of whether goals were achieved (Lee and Johnson 1983) or assessments of the effect of proposed policies. In Kansas, for example, the Legislative Division of Post Audit's report on the effect of eliminating university degrees and programs examined each university's degree programs and noted the reasons for discontinuing programs or degrees and the effects of the changes on resources (Green and Riggs 1988).

Technology and knowledge. A recent technological change that has affected budgeting is the widespread use of computers by staff and decision makers themselves. Most states have computerized data bases to permit tracking of the budget (both during development and execution) as well as links among agencies and higher education institutions (Adams 1988; Paterson 1985). Technology alone is only a portion of the total picture: Decision makers and others in the organization must be able to use the technology and must have an understanding of the issues related to the budget itself. Technological expenses in government are estimated to be 80 percent "orgware," that is, the people-oriented organizational issues that must be dealt with if a technological system is to be effective (Toregas 1988).

The relationship between the state and institutional funding

The most direct and tangible link between state government and higher education is usually the budget, and that relationship between state government and institutions of higher education shapes both the structure of the budget and its purposes (D. Jones 1984). A suggested spectrum of state-institutional funding relationships (termed "financial governance" to distinguish it from structural governance, which reflects discernible linear relationships [Curry and Fischer 1986]) ranges from educational institutions treated very much like state agencies to institutions that function like independent, nonprofit organizations and get funds through contract for service (Curry, Fischer, and Jons 1982). In between these two ends of the spectrum are state-controlled institutions and state-aided institutions (see figure 2).

FIGURE 2

RELATIONSHIPS IN GOVERNANCE

State-Agency Model	State-Controlled Institution	State-Aided Institution	Independent (Free-Market) Institution

```
-------------------------   Greater Institutional Autonomy   ------------------------->
<------------------------      Greater State Control          ------------------------
```

Source: Curry, Fischer, and Jons 1982.

The funding relationships are complex, and they differ from state to state (D. Jones 1984). One area of variation is the difference between statewide coordinating and governing boards. Statewide governing boards tend to be more concerned with issues of institutional management, whereas coordinating boards concern themselves with issues of higher education policy. Because of these differences, their approaches to budgeting for higher education could differ. No evidence of it exists in the literature, and it would be worthy of future study. Furthermore, the relationships can vary for different types of institutions within a state. "For example, in California, community colleges are treated as local governmental entities, while the university and state college and university systems are treated as state operations and subject to different budget procedures" (Curry and Fischer 1986, p. 11). In fact, some empirical support exists for at least differentiating state systems of two-year colleges on a continuum of financial and personnel regulation, much like that suggested by Curry and Fischer (Fonte 1989). In addition, the relationship within a state may change over time as a state loosens or tightens its control over institutions and their patterns of spending (Hines 1988a).

The Approach to Funding

The approach to funding itself is another major segment of the conceptual framework. Frequently, research on funding techniques has been too descriptive and less analytical than it could be. Such a focus may underemphasize some key issues, notably those associated with policy judgments and the decision process. Understanding and clarifying the decision process can be assisted by focusing not only on policy objectives or techniques but also on examining how those elements affect—or are affected by—criteria for evaluation.

Formula funding is the predominant approach to funding states use (Lamb 1986). A recent survey found that of 46 respondent states, 29 used a formula or guideline to request and/or allocate state general funds for public higher education (Maryland Higher Education Commission 1988). Within any approach to funding, certain policy judgments shape the particular technique of allocation used and some sort of evaluation of the utility of the approach.

Categories of policy judgments

Funding decisions are made on the basis of policy judgments that can be categorized in four ways: (1) the link between efficiency and enrollment, (2) diversity of missions, (3) equity and fair share, and (4) quality, outcomes, and effectiveness. Policy makers make choices among their values and set priorities as they develop—or use—an approach to allocation that handles the issues included in these categories. Whether objective (that is, quantitative) procedures and data are used does not alter the fact that policy makers make value decisions (Wirt, Mitchell, and Marshall 1988).

The link between efficiency and enrollment. Many funding decisions, especially those in states using formulas, are linked in some way to enrollment in higher education. These enrollment-based approaches to funding are legacies, many observers believe, of the growth era (Brinkman 1984; Caruthers and Orwig 1979; Hale and Rawson 1976; D. Jones 1984; Moss and Gaither 1976). In periods of growth, the real cost of one additional student, that is, the marginal cost to the institution, is less than the average cost of a student. In times of declining enrollment, institutions can incur disproportionate losses of funding if formula-based reductions are based on average costs. Approaches to funding that lessen the hold of enrollment over funding include decoupling, buffering, enrollment corridors, or marginal or fixed costs. "Decoupling" refers to shifting funding from enrollment-based approaches to program-based funding to remove enrollment as a source of reductions in funding. "Buffering" is used to smooth a precipitous drop in enrollment in a single year by averaging enrollments over several years. "Enrollment corridors" provide a range of allowable change that does not affect levels of funding. And approaches using "marginal or fixed costs" mitigate the effect of a decline in enrollments by reducing fewer resources than would be the case with a linear funding formula (Hines 1988a).

As states with funding formulas consider such approaches, two kinds of questions arise. The first has to do with the technical correctness of the approach, the second with whether the addition of complexity to the funding technique interferes with desirable procedural or process values. Decoupling, along with other recent changes, for example, had the disadvantage of making formulas much more complex (Brinkman 1984). Similarly, both questions of technical expertise and political problems stand in the way of states' widely adopting techniques of marginal costing (Allen and Topping 1979).

Diversity of mission. Diversity of educational mission is an underlying value of most state systems of higher education. The flagship research university has a different expected role and mission from that of the regional colleges or the community college system. Formula funding has often been criticized for having a "leveling" effect on institutions (Gross 1973), because formulas may fail to adequately recognize differences in mission.

Equity and fair share. One approach to equity or fairness in state government appropriations is providing the same funds to each institution for each FTE student enrolled in a comparable program of instruction. Equity or fair share focuses on several aspects of "fair share" in the division of funds. The "equity" or "fair share" in allocation is decided on the basis of divisions (1) of funds among institutions as well as divisions within institutions, (2) of costs between the student and the state (Hearn and Anderson 1989), and (3) of funds between the state and an institution's other sources of funds. The use of economic analysis in the calculation of "public benefit" and the division of state versus local or private shares has been suggested (Breneman and Nelson 1981). The "public benefit" is, however, ultimately "in the eyes of the beholder . . . [and] the evaluation is political" (p. 47).

Techniques of allocation
Techniques for allocating resources can be divided into two basic and competing approaches: (1) the political or interest group interaction model and (2) the "rational school" models (Morgan 1984). The former includes incrementalism and political log rolling, the latter formula funding as well as lesser-used approaches like zero-base budgeting (ZBB), planning programming and budgeting systems (PPBS), and performance budgeting. Despite their inclusion in the "rationalist" group, formulas are often "adjusted" for political reasons. Funding formulas are "a combination of technical judgments and political agreements" (Meisinger 1976, p. 2).

Formative and summative evaluation
Evaluative processes. State decision makers evaluate the process and results either explicitly or implicitly. A number of authors have described explicit evaluation, occurring while allocation is ongoing, in the literature on formula funding (Brinkman 1984; Caruthers and Orwig 1979; Hale and Rawson 1976; Halstead 1974; Morgan 1984; Moss and Gaither 1976).

The seminal work on state funding formulas provides three broad criteria for evaluating an approach to funding:

1. *Technical expertise.* Does the formal technique of allocation measure, weight, identify, or qualify effectively what it purports to measure, weight, identify, or qualify?
2. *Two-way feedback.* Is the allocation process "open" and does it encourage and facilitate participation and the communication of views on institutional needs and the state's priorities among all actors in the process (legislature, governor, higher education agency, institutions, the general public)?
3. *Clarification of values and issues.* To what extent does the allocation process highlight the choices in value and the facts involved in any choice? (Miller 1964).

Incentives . . . are thought to be more efficient in achieving objectives than are regulations.

Formative and summative evaluation provides opportunities to assess both the process and the outcomes and to modify either or both. Because state appropriations are made through overlapping cycles, the results of summative evaluation can be used as formative evaluation and feed immediately into the process. Unfortunately, evaluation of state funding processes is one of the less fully developed parts of the decision process, and the opportunity is not fully exploited.

Quality, outcomes, and effectiveness. In most states, the maintenance of quality is the responsibility of the institutions. Increasingly, however, states have attempted to define and use some measure of quality in their funding procedures, though most have found it difficult to define or measure. The absence of performance criteria in past approaches to allocation is "not a matter of simple oversight" (Folger 1984, p. 2). States wishing to include criteria for quality or performance in the budget process must deal with the definitions of quality and effectiveness, the measurement of performance, and the establishment of objectives for quality or performance. The practice of measuring and recognizing quality in higher education spread rapidly through states in the 1980s. A survey of the 50 states in 1983 showed that for four-year colleges and universities, 13 states were specifically "changing their financing structure to promote quality" (Leslie 1983, p. 187). A more recent survey found that almost half of the states now have explicit incentives in their budget processes to improve the quality of higher education (Maryland Higher Education Commission 1988). States have increased the use of incentives for at least two reasons: Incentives are part of a "market strategy" of voluntary participation by colleges and universities, and they are thought to be more efficient in achieving objectives than are regulations (Folger 1989). States recognize other outcomes: number of degrees granted, for which they might allocate money on the basis of reimbursement, or increased enrollment or retention of minority students.

Research questions arising from this category are similar to those recognizing mission: an analysis of trade-offs of institutional autonomy, communication of values, and consideration of whether the process is participatory.

Summary
Examination of the state higher education budget process begins with a state's external environment, which includes its history, politics, economy, and demography. The effects of these major factors have been studied with respect to the total budgetary outcome of total spending on higher education. Their effects are varied, in part because the research varies in approaches used. The effects also vary because different states have different environments at different times and respond differently to environmental conditions. The state filters the environment somewhat as it responds to, or ignores, environmental factors.

The roles of various organizational participants depend on the state in which they are working. In most states, the governor sets the broad agenda or parameters of the state's budget, and the legislature modifies the distribution of the budget. Governors' budget offices are also important participants; however, their roles and influence are little studied phenomena. These roles are both informal and formal, the latter including styles of financial governance.

Budgets operate on several time schedules, including four phases in a single budget cycle: preparation, approval, execution, and audit. Each phase is affected by changes in technology and knowledge, the most obvious of which is the spreading use of computers. Budget preparation and allocation involve various techniques of funding, such as formulas, which are the most common approach states use. A phase undergoing substantial change is evaluation and feedback. States increasingly use this phase of the budget process as a means to promote and study quality and effectiveness in higher education.

THE ENVIRONMENTAL CONTEXT OF BUDGETING

Why do some states spend over $200 per person in state revenue on higher education, while others spend barely $100 per person (see table 2)? And why do some states appropriate $15 or more per $1,000 of income, while other states spend less than $8 per $1,000 of income? One factor contributing to these wide variations among states is the special external environment affecting each state. The impact of the external environment on state appropriations for higher education is significant (Layzell 1988b; Lyddon 1989). The external environment does not fully explain the variances in funding for higher education among the states, however.

TABLE 2

APPROPRIATIONS OF STATE TAX FUNDS FOR HIGHER EDUCATION OPERATING EXPENSES PER CAPITA AND PER $1,000 OF PERSONAL INCOME: FISCAL YEAR 1990

	State Tax Appropriations ($000)	Appropriation per Capita		Appropriation per $1,000 of Income	
		Amount	*Rank*	*Amount*	*Rank*
Alaska	$176,023	$311.55	1	$17.59	2
Hawaii	292,456	260.89	2	15.90	4
Wyoming	116,183	230.98	3	17.81	1
North Carolina	1,458,516	220.92	4	15.71	6
Minnesota	946,779	220.28	5	13.19	11
North Dakota	139,911	210.71	6	16.34	3
California	5,740,737	200.68	7	10.81	19
Alabama	776,641	187.14	8	14.73	8
New Mexico	296,410	185.84	9	15.75	5
Nebraska	290,491	182.70	10	12.27	13
Virginia	1,107,480	182.51	11	10.42	25
Iowa	502,293	180.68	12	12.09	14
New York	3,185,045	179.33	13	9.21	35
Kansas	444,788	178.99	14	11.31	17
Maryland	823,348	176.49	15	9.14	37
Delaware	115,541	175.59	16	9.91	28
South Carolina	612,508	174.65	17	13.66	9
Washington	790,383	171.38	18	10.32	26
Wisconsin	784,141	165.60	19	10.55	23
Mississippi	432,971	161.56	20	14.87	7
Idaho	158,247	156.22	21	12.46	12
Arizona	569,982	156.20	22	10.91	18
Utah	272,201	155.54	23	13.21	10

TABLE 2 (continued)

APPROPRIATIONS OF STATE TAX FUNDS FOR HIGHER EDUCATION OPERATING EXPENSES

	State Tax Appropriations ($000)	Appropriation per Capita		Appropriation per $1,000 of Income	
		Amount	Rank	Amount	Rank
Michigan	$1,408,009	$151.95	24	$ 9.21	36
Texas	2,624,288	150.38	25	10.68	21
Colorado	504,757	148.76	26	9.29	34
Tennessee	727,449	147.47	27	10.71	20
Kentucky	550,182	147.03	28	11.51	15
Maine	176,868	147.02	29	9.71	30
Indiana	814,021	146.88	30	9.82	29
New Jersey	1,142,805	146.01	31	6.73	47
Rhode Island	144,522	145.10	32	8.62	39
Illinois	1,675,322	144.44	33	8.21	41
Oregon	395,898	143.96	34	9.61	32
Connecticut	463,796	142.40	35	6.22	49
Nevada	146,636	139.79	36	7.94	42
Massachusetts	815,998	139.18	37	6.66	48
Oklahoma	453,090	137.93	38	10.49	24
Georgia	884,669	135.60	39	9.14	38
Montana	109,416	135.42	40	10.57	22
West Virginia	251,505	134.42	41	11.42	16
Ohio	1,427,041	132.29	42	8.46	40
Florida	1,567,712	125.07	43	7.66	43
Arkansas	301,200	124.77	44	10.29	27
South Dakota	85,995	121.46	45	9.46	33
Missouri	603,535	116.90	46	7.60	44
Louisiana	522,912	115.95	47	9.65	31
Pennsylvania	1,361,361	114.94	48	6.99	46
Vermont	59,936	107.61	49	7.03	45
New Hampshire	74,393	66.66	50	3.53	50
Total	**$39,326,391**	**$159.18**		**$9.74**	

Source: Grapevine, December 1989, No. 359, p. 2270.

The focus of this section is the environmental context within which the state budget process for higher education operates and within which policy makers and practitioners must function. It discusses the interrelated aspects of the changing external environment—historical traditions and the political, economic, and demographic contexts—and the resulting challenges for practitioners and state policy makers.

Historical Traditions

A central function of all political systems is to allocate resources among competing preferences for their use (Wirt, Mitchell, and Marshall 1988). Values and policy preferences are at the heart of all state budget processes. Participants in a state's budget process bring with them the values and policy preferences of their constituencies—state agencies, interest groups, and, of course, private citizens—which are both conflicting and complementary, narrowly defined and wide ranging. In short, the spectrum of values and policy preferences represented in the state budget process mirrors that within the state's citizenry. "If politics is regarded as conflict over whose preferences are to prevail in the determination of policy, then the budget records the outcomes of this struggle" (Wildavsky 1986, p. 9). From one perspective, then, a state's annual or biennial budget effectively summarizes the values and policy preferences present within the state culture as conveyed by the participants in the budget process.

The dimension of value

The current values and preferences in any state's culture about areas of public policy, such as higher education, have not been generated within a vacuum. They are rather the result of deeply held historical traditions passed from generation to generation, which could be either beliefs or practices (Fisher 1988a). Further, these traditions may be nebulous, as in the case of myths and sagas (for example, the ongoing attempt by some to maintain Virginia Military Institute as an all-male institution), or they may be quantifiable, as in the case of constitutional articles or state statutes. Regardless of their source, these traditions frame the state's higher education policy/budget process and act as behavioral regulators for the participants. One dimension of historical traditions can be termed the "value dimension." "Value" in this context is meant in the collective sense, as opposed to individual philosophical values. The collective value historically accorded to education by the residents of a state significantly affects state educational policy making and expenditures (Wirt and Kirst 1972). Patterns of public spending for education (that is, resources allocated among competing preferences) tend to be affected by a state's historical traditions as well. For example, states with historically strong private sectors of higher education tend to spend less over time on public

higher education relative to public education for kindergarten through grade 12 (Garms 1986).

The dimension of control

Control is another historical dimension of the state policy/budget process for higher education. In earlier days, the relationship between higher education and state government was one-sided. Colleges and universities kept state government at arm's length until it was time for more funding (D. Jones 1984). Early American colleges "considered themselves private foundations. They accepted public grants, to be sure, but never surrendered control [to the state] over policy formation . . ." (Brubacher and Rudy 1976, p. 35). In fact, until the passage of the Morrill Act, the establishment of colleges was predominantly a function of private groups.

This arrangement did not last. As the number of higher education institutions in this country grew during the 20th century, so did the number of state-level coordinating and governing boards. A comparative analysis of legislation passed in four states between 1900 and 1979 found that over time the amount of legislation affecting higher education increased (Fisher 1988b). A tendency did not exist, however, to restrict institutional autonomy (Fisher 1988b). Rather, the sheer growth over time in these regulatory mechanisms has led to increased perceptions of reduced autonomy by the academy. These perceptions are not without warrant. As governors, legislatures, and the general public have become more sophisticated about higher education, the desire for greater control during and after the budget process has also increased (Hines 1988a). Further, although the American legal system has been—and remains—highly receptive to the concept of "corporate" autonomy from external control, over time the academic profession has become fragmented with regard to the principles that underlie academic freedom (Leslie 1987). This fact too encourages outside intervention.

The Political Context

Closely related to the context of historical traditions is the political context. "The social life of a citizen is interwoven into the political life, and the mediating factor that makes [it] possible is culture" (Wirt, Mitchell, and Marshall 1988, p. 271). Higher education and state politics have been intertwined since the Massachusetts legislature began making direct legislative grants to Harvard in the 1600s (Brubacher and Rudy 1976). In later years, the passage of the Morrill Act ensured that higher education would remain within the realm of state politics indefinitely (Hines and Hartmark 1980). Three aspects of the changing political environment as it relates to state budgeting for higher education include the structure of higher education, gubernatorial influence, and legislative influence.

The structure of higher education

During the 1960s and 1970s, most of the states established coordinating agencies to handle the massive expansion higher education was experiencing at that time (McGuinness 1988). With the formation of these state agencies, many of the powers previously accorded institutional governing boards transferred to the agencies, including planning, budgetary, and financial functions. All states, with the exception of Wyoming, have a statutory state-level coordinating, governing, and/or planning board for higher education. Of these states, 43 have statutory authority to review and/or recommend budgets for higher education to the governor or legislature (McGuinness 1988).

The extent to which these state coordinating or governing entities share authority in the state budget process, both formal/ex officio and informal, depends greatly on the state's political culture. These relationships have a significant, although not always obvious, effect on the conception and implementation of the budget (D. Jones 1984). And these relationships vary from state to state: "The conditions of each state determine form and powers" (Glenny 1985, p. 13).

Much of this variance can be explained by the degree of centralization present in the state's structure of higher education. Figure 2, in the previous section, presents a useful continuum for analyzing the degree of centralization within a higher education structure. It shows four structural models, ranging from the highly centralized to the highly decentralized. In the *state-agency model*, the coordinating agency and the legislature make all of the budget decisions for the institutions and exercise strict financial control over them. In the *state-controlled model*, the coordinating agency, although still the primary authority for higher education, relies more on the budget requests of the institutions than in the state-agency model. In the *state-aided model*, the state and the institution are jointly responsible for the financing of the institution, and the coordinating agency tends to be more of an adviser than an authority. And in the *free-market model,* the institution is financially responsible for itself, and the state contracts with the institution to provide educational services to the citizens of the state. In this situation, the coordinating agency is but a conduit for the appropriated funds and has no real influence in the budget process. In reality, none of these models exist in their pure state (D. Jones 1984). In fact, virtually all of the states fall into one of the first three models (Volkwein 1987). This continuum illustrates, however, how the roles, responsibilities, and influence of the coordinating agency and the governing board in the budget process can vary according to the structure in place.

Despite the difference of the structural conditions within each state, a common element of tension remains between coordinating agencies and governing boards. In recent years, this tension has formed along what can be termed the "accountability/autonomy axis." As state budgets have become tighter and more competitive, higher education's constituencies have become more insistent about seeing real outcomes from public dollars (Floyd 1982). Although the term "accountability" is most often discussed in a fiscal context, it in fact has a much broader meaning. The concept of accountability has many different facets affecting different policy domains, including the more common concept of fiscal accountability (Hartmark and Hines 1986). Accordingly, the term "accountability" can connote different principles to different constituencies at the same time.

In many states, the coordinating agency is the gateway to higher education and thus becomes the sounding board and messenger for these constituencies. The message that coordinating agencies have been bringing to the campuses is that they must be accountable in all policy domains. Over time, the mechanisms used for ensuring accountability have ranged from the formal (for example, statute, performance audit, and administrative rules) to the informal (political clout) (Mingle and Lenth 1989).

At the other side of this axis is the issue of institutional autonomy. The academy has held sacred the principles of institutional self-governance or self-determination throughout history. At the core of these principles lie the concepts of academic freedom and tenure (Leslie 1987). The advent of coordinating agencies and increased state regulation of insti-

tutional matters has led to feelings on campus of overin-
trusiveness by these agencies into institutional matters. Although legislation related to higher education has increased
over time, no evidence exists that actual institutional autonomy has been restricted (Fisher 1988b). In legal matters surrounding academic freedom and "corporate autonomy," the
courts have generally deferred to the rights of the institution to exercise its judgment in all matters related to the
institution:

> *The Supreme Court has clearly articulated the fundamental*
> *rationale for its [corporate autonomy] existence on several*
> *occasions. To wit: a university is held to exist for the purpose*
> *of advancing the free pursuit of ideas and enjoys some*
> *measure of First Amendment respect, if not direct protec-*
> *tion, as an instrument for the advancement of this basic*
> *social value* (Leslie 1987, pp. 300–301).

It appears, then, that institutional autonomy remains intact.

In the political sphere, however, perceptions are reality.
The call for increased measures of accountability for higher
education has increased the feeling of diminished autonomy
to the point of supersensitivity on both sides. An example
of this tension recently took place in Vermont. In response
to increased public feelings that the University of Vermont
had lost sight of its mission to the citizens of the state, the
legislature requested that the university show how its research
benefited the state and that decisions about faculty tenure
were justified. In response, the chairman of the university's
board of trustees sent back a "scorching reply to this assault
upon 200 years of academic autonomy" (*Economist* 1989b,
p. 28). In short, although autonomy may not in reality be diminished, it is perceived to be so and thus external demands
for institutional accountability are being met with increased
hostility.

Gubernatorial influence
Over time, governors have begun to take a more active role
in the formation of policy for higher education (Herzik 1988).
Over the past several years, the impetus for creating policy
for higher education has shifted from institutions to the executive mansion (Adler and Lane 1988). In fact, "no single
individual is more important to the development of higher

education in any state than the governor" (p. 10). While the validity of this claim may vary from state to state, it is generally true that the governor has the formal authority to veto or sign legislation, appoint his or her own people to state and institutional coordinating and governing boards, and recommend a budget for higher education (Beyle 1983). In essence, the governor's main role in the budget process is that of chief facilitator. An important original study of the politics of the higher education budget process found the governor indeed to be playing a leading role in the formation of the higher education budget in Michigan, Wisconsin, and Illinois (Lingenfelter 1974). Of course, this role is played out through formal powers, personal charisma, and a host of other intangible factors. Indeed, one governor in a southern state who lacked formal powers achieved significant changes in education through shrewd negotiation, consensus building, and example (Kearney 1987). It seems valid to assert that "it is the governor who has the greatest potential to become the initiator as well as the catalyst for policy changes" in higher education (Adler and Lane 1988, p. 17). From the perspective of one former executive officer in state higher education from the Northwest, the role of the governor in higher education policy making may have become too active (see Davis 1988a). He lost his job as a result of the new governor's strong interest in higher education policy.

The governor does not make recommendations without help. Virtually all governors have an executive budget office, and over one-third of all governors have their own appointed aides for education and higher education (Davis 1988b). These professional staffers know the political economy of the state well and in particular the financial outlook for the coming fiscal year. They "protect the governor from midyear changes in spending plans or from ending up with deficits" (Albritton and Dran 1987, p. 145). This trend in the professionalization of the executive branch has intensified in recent years (Hines 1988a), and, as such, the executive budget staff and higher education aides are the individuals on whom the governor increasingly relies for setting spending limits and developing priorities in preparing budget recommendations.

Legislative influence
The relationship between higher education and state government became increasingly complex throughout the 1980s

(McGuinness 1986). This increased complexity has resulted in legislatures that are more sophisticated in matters of higher education policy than were their predecessors in many cases (McGuinness 1986). Further, the legislature has moved from a minor to a major player in the formation of policy for higher education. One reason for it is the fact that for many states, higher education has become the largest discretionary item in the budget (Zusman 1986). This increase in state expenditures on higher education has increased the interest of legislators into how and where those funds are spent.

This is where the similarity between the executive and the legislative branches ends, however. Two primary factors contribute to the different type of influence that the legislature exerts on the budget process for higher education. The first factor, which could be termed the "constituency factor," is based on the premise that while the governor must be the archetypal statesman representing the wide spectrum of public concern within the state, individual legislators must put first the concerns of the voters in their own particular districts (Brandl 1988). In other words, legislators are the ultimate purveyors of Tip O'Neill's maxim that "all politics is local." Legislators push those expenditures that directly benefit their districts and are indifferent—or worse—toward those budget items that result in little or no benefit for the home district (Wildavsky 1986), and a legislator whose district includes a college or university will be more likely to favor expenditures benefiting the institution and higher education in general (Brandl 1988).

The second factor could be termed the "party-affiliation factor." The two-party structure inherent in the American political system typically fosters intense party loyalties and interparty competition that become readily apparent in the budget process. Each party seeks to maximize its presence in the state and as a result aligns itself with popular issues as a source of symbolic identification. Each party elevates its own proposed policies and denigrates the others, regardless of the budgetary ramifications (Wildavsky 1986). Legislators, then, must support their party's position on specific policy matters as well as constituents' interests. Party affiliation is also important in determining key committee assignments and leadership (Lingenfelter 1974).

The legislature serves a dual role in the higher education budget process. On the one hand, as watchers of the public

Each party elevates its own proposed policies and denigrates the others, regardless of the budgetary ramifications.

purse, legislators act as stewards of funds for higher education. The legislature must ensure that public funds are spent efficiently and effectively. On the other hand, the legislature also serves as the forum for constituents' and the party's policy preferences. In a sense, these roles are mutually exclusive in that one role requires that rational spending decisions be made while the other is inherently irrational, forsaking sound fiscal policy in an effort to satisfy a multitude of needs and desires (Brandl 1988). "Intense party competition and high voter turnout often work in favor of high expenditures" (Sharkansky, cited in Wildavsky 1986, p. 236). In the legislative session in spring 1989, after the speaker of the House and the Senate president (both Democrats) backed a tax increase for education (see Cage 1989a), the four main partisan groups within the Illinois General Assembly (that is, House Democrats, House Republicans, Senate Democrats, and Senate Republicans) each introduced separate new spending plans for higher education, each one progressively larger than the other.

Like the governor, the legislature has a staff to attend to the budget and to substantive policy issues. Over the past 40 years, these staffs have become more professional and predominant in the budget process (Pipho 1988). The roles of these staffs may range from nonpartisan analyst to political aide and cover all points in between, depending on the state. In Florida, for example, the nonpartisan higher education budget analysts in both the House and the Senate review the entire higher education budget request and then make a formal presentation of their recommendations to their respective committees (Turnbull and Irvin 1984). In Illinois, staffers are partisan and more politically active and tend to be less conspicuous in the formal areas of the budget process. Despite this variance, all state legislative staff have become what one observer once predicted they would become: "anonymous leaders of higher education" (Glenny 1972).

The Economic Context

If historical traditions set the stage and politics provides the actors, then the economic context writes the script that frames the budget outcome for higher education at the state level. "Not only does higher education affect economic prosperity and the entire macroeconomic environment but that environment [also] has a very direct impact on the operation of our institutions of higher learning" (Anderson and Massy

1989, p. 2). During the 1980s, this observation was illustrated in different regions of the country in that the states with the greatest increase in state tax support for higher education were located in regions of the country with the strongest economies and vice versa (Hines, Hickrod, and Pruyne 1989). Three interrelated aspects of the economic context affect state budgeting for higher education: general economic conditions, state tax capacity, and availability of state revenues.

General economic conditions

Public support for higher education is directly related to the general condition of a state's economy (Wittstruck and Bragg 1988). Nationally, the economy has enjoyed a period of sustained expansion since 1982, with just a few states the exceptions. In the wake of this expansion, the United States has been involved in a balancing act, trying to prevent inflation from skyrocketing or recession from occurring (Anderson and Massy 1989). Either one of these events could trigger severe budget problems for higher education. High inflation lowers real faculty salaries, lowers available federal funds for research and student aid, and adversely affects endowments (Anderson 1988b). On the other hand, the onset of recession could reduce state tax yields, resulting in depleted state general fund reserves (Carnevale 1988), which, in turn, could bring about a period of fiscal stringency and retrenchment like that seen in the early 1980s (Gold 1987).

Two aspects of the economy that affect state budgeting and bear special mention are the state unemployment rate and the per capita income rate. All things being equal, a low unemployment rate is a prime indicator of a healthy economy. Conversely, states with high unemployment rates typically have a high degree of competing demands placed upon a shrinking state budget, which directly affects the share going to higher education (Gold 1987). High unemployment creates an increased need for state services, such as public aid and other social services. Paradoxically, one of the benefits derived from higher education is a more competent and employable work force (Johnston and Associates 1987). Some state policy makers have realized this relationship, even in the face of dismal state economies. "To neglect education this year, based on the premise that the economy is bad . . . saves money in the short run but is a disastrous decision in the long run" (Nebraska Gov. Kerrey, cited in Beyle 1985, p. 49). Despite this

recognition on the part of state policy makers, the reality of the situation is that unemployment decreases the availability of state revenues and increases competition for the remaining state funds.

One obvious reason for the relationship between the relative wealth of the population and the level of government expenditures (Wildavsky 1986) is that wealthier states have a greater tax base than do poorer states. Empirical research has indicated that a significant relationship exists between per capita income and state expenditures for higher education (Garms 1986). In fact, one group of researchers concluded that "per capita income is the most important single factor affecting higher education spending" (Kim and Price 1977, p. 260). A less obvious reason for this relationship is the fact that gross family income and a family's disposable income are directly related. The more income a family has, the more it can spend on "nonessentials" like higher education. Demand for higher education services is determined to some extent by affluence. Thus, as a state's per capita income increases, demand for these services increases, in turn putting pressure on state governments to increase their expenditures on higher education.

State tax capacity

State tax capacity is defined as the amount of state revenue that would be generated if the revenue base were tapped at the maximum allowable rates for taxes and service fees (Berne and Schramm 1986). Revenue bases include the volume of general sales, licenses issued, corporate income, personal income, property value, and oil and gas production (Halstead 1989b). For comparative purposes, if uniform tax rates are applied to every state's revenue base, a wide variance exists among states (Halstead 1989b). Thus, the most important variable in determining the level of a state's tax capacity is not the nominal tax rates but the underlying economic activity. And "state governments face no more severe handicap in their task of adequately supporting public services than the near permanent burden of low tax capacity" (p. 22). Not surprisingly, states with higher tax capacities have been shown to allot more state revenue to higher education than states with low tax capacities (Garms 1986).

To improve tax capacity, some states opt to raise taxes. With the advent of revenue shortfalls, many states, both high and low capacity, have opted to increase tax rates to make up revenue (Gold 1987). The primary effect that economic activity has on a state's tax capacity and on resulting expenditures should not be underestimated, however. Louisiana has long relied on the oil and gas industries in the state to provide revenues for public services. In 1982, 41 percent of the state's revenues came directly from oil and gas (*Economist* 1989a). When the oil and gas industries began to dry up, however, so did Louisiana's revenue base, resulting in a $700 million budget deficit in 1989 (Cage 1989b). As a result, Louisiana Governor Buddy Roemer threatened that unless changes in the state tax structure were made to shift more of the burden to individuals and away from the faltering oil and gas industries, at least half of the state's public universities would have to be closed (Cage 1989b). State voters, however, defeated a constitutional amendment to implement these changes in the state tax structure (Pipho 1989). This example illustrates not only the importance of the state's economy on tax capacity but also the political dynamic that occurs within state fiscal policy.

In some states, governors have realized that improving tax capacity is more effectively achieved through economic development than through tax increases (Hines 1988a). Higher education has been seen as a means for improving the economic base, primarily through development of high technology. Several states have developed plans to entice high-technology industries to establish or relocate within their borders by using higher education as a large part of the bait (Johnson 1984). In Illinois, both public and private institutions of higher education have established academic centers in the western suburbs of Chicago to offer graduate studies to residents and to encourage high-technology development (Keenan 1987). Working in conjunction with private industry, Florida has established "centers of excellence" and other research initiatives at universities. Higher education is also involved in training and retraining the work force, which also benefits the economy and ultimately tax capacity. Between 1985 and 1989, the state of Ohio committed $8.8 million in its Productivity Improvement Challenge to provide incentives for community colleges, technical colleges, and university regional colleges to develop approaches to increase the participation of state residents in higher education, job training, and retraining (Ohio Board of Regents 1989). As higher education becomes more involved with improving the state economic base, it is likely that even more benefits will accrue to colleges and universities. Evidence is found in the fact that many states with large increases in appropriations for higher education during the latter part of the 1980s explicitly linked higher education with economic development (Hines, Hickrod, and Pruyne 1989).

Availability of state revenues

Closely related to state tax capacity is the availability of state revenues. The principal difference between strong and weak state support of higher education is the availability of state revenues (Hines, Hickrod, and Pruyne 1989). Availability of revenues is simply the amount of current and projected revenue growth expected in the next budget period. A survey of state-level budget officers in five western states indicated that a majority felt that availability of revenues was the major factor affecting budget decisions in their states (Duncombe and Kinney 1986). A major reason is that, unlike the federal government, most state governments are required to operate within balanced budgets. Several researchers have analyzed the relationship between availability of state revenues and state expenditures for higher education and found significant relationships (see, e.g., Coughlin and Erekson 1986; Garms 1986). Further, although availability of revenues is important, the willingness of lawmakers to spend it on higher education is even more crucial (Hines, Hickrod, and Pruyne 1989). Additional state revenues do not benefit higher education if they are not directed toward higher education.

An interesting twist on this factor is the current situation in California. Until recently, state spending for higher education was regulated by the "Gann limit," which limited the growth of state expenditures to a function of growth in state population and inflation, with the predominant factor being growth in population. If the demand for services is greater than population growth, funds would have to be reallocated or services curtailed. Currently, the state's higher education system is experiencing substantial growth in enrollments, which is projected to increase by 2.4 percent annually, while state population is projected to grow by only 1.5 percent annually between 1988 and 2005 (California Postsecondary Education Commission 1990). As a result of this growth, the University of California projects the need for three new campuses, the California State University system projects the need for expansion at its 20 existing campuses, and the community college system may need as many as 23 new campuses. In 1990, however, Californians voted to raise the spending limit through a measure known as Proposition 111, which relieves the fiscal pressure on the state's three-tiered system of higher education, at least for the present (*Chronicle* 1990). Other state budget categories, with the exception of kindergarten through grade 12 and community colleges for which the Gann limit was originally lifted, also face growing caseloads.

An issue affecting many states in the 1980s was the problem of declining available revenues and increasing demands from other areas of state government, such as public aid and corrections (Pipho 1989). As a result, the dynamic that occurred within higher education (especially public higher education) is that tuition was increased to make up for lost state revenues. Not surprisingly, over time an inverse relationship occurs between state appropriations for public institutions and public tuition levels (Wittstruck and Bragg 1988). In the early 1980s when the economy was in a recession, growth in state funding for higher education was limited, and tuition at public institutions went through a period of double-digit increases. When the economy improved, however, growth in tuition was limited (Hauptman 1989). Interestingly, large increases in tuition occur when the economy is doing poorly and students can least afford to pay, but when the economy is doing well, tuition is kept stable (Hauptman 1989). In sum, shortfalls and competing demands on state revenues have a double impact on higher education. Not only do revenue shortages force higher education to increase tuition; many students also will not be able to pay the increases.

The Demographic Context
A state's demographic context affects the state budget outcome in that the mix of population and overall growth or decline directly affects services required. State demographics affect higher education at both a macro- and a microlevel. At the macrolevel, changes in overall population and in the composition of the population, such as age and minority distribution, affect the demand for different types of public services, such as higher education. At a microlevel, changes in patterns and participation rates in higher education affect policy makers' perceived need of higher education.

Changes in the overall population

It has been argued that changes in overall state population affect both the overall state budget process (Wildavsky 1986) and the state budget process for higher education (Lyddon, Fonte, and Miller 1987; Volkwein 1987). If population levels increase, the need for state services increases correspondingly. If population levels decrease, then corresponding economic difficulties usually require a cutback in state services. An analysis of two-year changes in appropriations for higher education indicates a positive relationship between the geographic location of a state and a change in the level of appropriations for higher education (Hines 1988b). States in areas undergoing large increases in population, such as the Sunbelt, have tended to show large increases in appropriations for higher education, while states whose populations are stagnant or declining (the Midwest, for example) have tended to show little or even negative growth in appropriations for higher education. Again, growth in overall state population usually requires that the state's service delivery systems be expanded and vice versa.

Changes in the composition of the population

Changes in the composition of the population also affect the state budget process, particularly the age distribution of the population and the percentage of minorities within the population. In general, our population is aging. Older citizens require different kinds of services from younger citizens. During the baby boom, when the younger, school-age cohort was expanding at a rate much faster than the rest of the population, state educational expenditures increased rapidly as well (Bowman 1985). Over a 30-year period, the numbers of a state's residents aged 5 to 17 and 18 to 20 were significant determinants of public revenues allocated to kindergarten through grade 12 and higher education in years when those age groups constituted a large percentage of the state's total population (Garms 1986). As the younger cohorts have declined as a percentage of the population, however, so has the significance of these relationships. On the other hand, older, "nontraditional" students have accounted for the majority of the growth in higher education enrollments in recent years (Frances 1986). These individuals typically enroll part time and require different services from traditional students, resulting in different kinds and levels of costs (Brinkman 1988).

Another pressure affecting the state higher education budget process is the changing minority population. During the 1980s, minorities accounted for the majority of the population growth in the United States (Johnston and Associates 1987). The pressure from this growth, however, is not that minority enrollments are increasing but that they are decreasing (Frances 1986). Further, minority students' achievement at all levels of education has, on average, been poor. In some states, these decreases and poor performance have resulted in strong political pressures on higher education from powerful minority legislators and their caucuses. As we approach the 21st century, the movement of our economy from a manufacturing to a technology and service base will mean that the majority of the new jobs created will require greater skills and education than currently (Johnston and Associates 1987).

The role of the legislature . . . is fueled more by provincialism and party politics than statesmanship.

Enrollment levels and participation rates

Traditionally, funding for higher education, at least as far as the operating budget is concerned, has been linked to enrollments (Leslie and Ramey 1986). More funding is appropriated as enrollment levels increase and vice versa. Enrollments have been considered to be such an integral factor in the higher education budget process that "with enrollments falling and competing demands for state services increasing, public higher education will find it difficult to get the appropriations it seeks" (Crosson 1983, p. 533). Conversely, states whose systems of higher education have been experiencing growth in enrollments should also be experiencing similar growth in appropriations, as in California.

Interestingly, evidence suggests that the traditional relationship between increased enrollments and increased appropriations is diminishing in importance. This relationship certainly was not the case in California until the 1990 passage of Proposition 111. A recent analysis found that increasing enrollments in public colleges and universities typically resulted in a net loss in state appropriations per FTE student. One reason for this phenomenon may be the political appeal of reducing enrollments to improve educational quality. Those institutions that pursue such a policy may fare better in the budget process than those that have uncontrolled growth in enrollments (Leslie and Ramey 1986).

Closely related to levels of enrollment is the state higher education participation rate, generally defined as the proportion of enrolled students to the college-aged cohort within the state; it is a measure of demand for higher education and to some extent the value residents place on higher education. Available data suggest that states with high participation rates in public higher education allocate a larger portion of their budget to public higher education (Halstead 1989b). During the 1980s, the ratio of public higher education FTE students to the 18- to 44-year-old population in the United States declined (Caruthers and Marks 1988). Part of the reason is the growth in older part-time students as a percentage of total enrollments. Over time, the growth in the participation rate of students aged 25 and older has increased (Frances 1986). These pressures on the participation rate may alter its impact in years to come.

Summary

The environmental context within which the state higher education budget process operates is multifaceted. Historical traditions, politics, economics, and demographics all underlie the values and policy preferences that participants bring with them to the process. These traditions frame the actions and interactions of the participants in often subtle ways.

Values and preferences are played out within the state's political context. Three major aspects of the political context are the structure of higher education, gubernatorial influence, and legislative influence. The structure of higher education within a state determines the extent to which the power of higher education in the budget process is centralized (that is, concentrated within a coordinating agency) or decentralized (that is, concentrated within individual institutions). Despite the structure of higher education in a state, a common element of tension exists between the state and institutional governing boards along the "accountability/autonomy" axis. Other increasing pressures within the political context include the increased role of the governor. Governors are taking more of a lead in setting the policy agendas for higher education that are played out in the budget process. The role of the legislature in the process is also increasing, although in general this role is fueled more by provincialism and party politics than statesmanship.

From an economic standpoint, general economic conditions, state tax capacity, and availability of state revenues all affect the process. Support for higher education is directly related to the general condition of a state's economy, including the level of inflation, per capita income, and unemployment rates. Also directly related to the state's economic condition is the state tax capacity, which is the maximum amount of revenue that would be generated if the revenue base were tapped at the maximum allowable tax rates. If the underlying economic base is poor, then tax capacity will be minimal. States with higher tax capacities generally allot more state revenue per capita to higher education than those with low capacities. In some states, governors have been attempting to improve tax capacity, not through increased tax rates but through economic development. Often, higher education is part of such efforts. Related to tax capacity is the availability of state revenues. Higher education's share of the budget is directly related to the level of state revenue available. In years when state revenues have been scarce, tuition has been increased at public institutions in many states to compensate for the shortfall.

Demographics are also an important pressure on the process. The level and composition of a state's population directly affect the services residents require. If the population increases, the level of state services required usually increases as well and vice versa. Further, the composition of the state's population affects the mix of services required. Data indicate that the population is growing older and the number of minorities is increasing. These trends will affect both the general state budget process and the specific area of higher education, as society strives to meet the special needs of these subpopulations. Enrollment in higher education and states' participation rates in higher education have traditionally been important factors in determining the level of funding provided to higher education, because both of them measure demand for higher education services. Recent analyses indicate, however, that the significance of these factors in the process may be decreasing.

THE BUDGETARY PROCESS

As shown, contextual factors in state budgeting for higher education are changing. The process itself is also changing—in the increasing number of actors and the roles they play, in structural issues, such as state-level governance and coordination of higher education, in timing issues, such as the advent of midyear reductions and supplemental appropriations, in creative financing techniques, and in strategies to allocate resources. Many of these issues have been referred to in the description of the budgeting framework and with regard to the environmental context. Portions of the process illustrated in the framework, however, are distinctive and deserve further discussion. Some portions of the higher education budgeting process at the state level are poorly supported with empirical research. One must then rely on research about other levels of government (such as federal or municipal governments) or research about budgeting for other state functions (such as elementary and secondary education, or general government).

Drawing precise conclusions about the nature of the state budgeting process for higher education is difficult for several reasons. Relying on studies conducted primarily about other levels of government is faulty, because the nature of authority is different in each level of government. For example, state governors usually have veto power over line items, allowing them to annul certain legislative decisions. The President lacks this authority in his relations with the U.S. Congress. Mayors or municipal managers are usually the dominant figures in their arenas, working with a weak or unassuming council (Wildavsky 1986).

Another difficulty with "borrowing" research is the nature of the relationship between state governments and colleges and universities. In some states, institutions might be treated for budgetary purposes much like other state departments. In other states, however, public colleges and universities operate much more like private institutions with which the state contracts for services (Curry and Fischer 1986). Clearly, the processes of budgeting for institutions under disparate conditions differ. Even within a single state, one system of higher education might be governed differently from another. In Michigan, for example, community colleges, with their locally elected boards and local taxing authority, are treated much like municipalities. They are considered local units of government for purposes of the state constitutional provision requiring a constant division in the state's budget between spending for state and local entities.

One reason for the scarcity of research about state government processes is the problem of dealing with more than 50 different sets of circumstances. "Studies about how budgetary decisions are made in states are scarce" (Wildavsky 1986, p. 222). Furthermore, budgetary processes are not static, so a study conducted 10 years ago may have little bearing on current budgeting processes. Changing conditions sometimes cause changes in budgeting processes, or vice versa. For example, budgeting under severe economic constraints differs from budgeting under conditions of greater flexibility:

> *The most important variable determining the behavior of participants is the adequacy of revenues. Since state budgets must be balanced and most expenses cannot be controlled, when revenues increase at a slower rate than spending, budgeting will become a form of revenue behavior. . . . When money comes in faster than it goes out, more options become available. Will the governor and the legislature seek economic growth so as to produce painless revenue, or will they generate political support to overcome resistance to higher taxation?* (Wildavsky 1986, p. 240).

Most budget cuts resulting from revenue shortfalls occur under emergency conditions; thus, an opportunity rarely occurs for planning by either states or institutions (National Conference 1982). Revenue shortfalls can result from downturns in the economy, failure of revenues to keep pace with inflation, reduced federal spending for state and local governments, tax revolts, or other reasons. Patterns of the growth of expenditures in states suggest that they (and local units of government) are "unable to substantially reduce expenditure growth in times of fiscal stress because of the difficulties associated with work force reductions or delaying spending on major contracts" (Carnevale 1988, p. 40).

Even with caveats about the research in mind, literature is available from which to learn about the process of state budgeting for higher education. The discussion begins with the link between the environmental context and the budget process, then moves through the framework for the budgetary process outlined earlier.

The Link between the Environmental Context and the Budget Process

Changing public attitudes about government spending in general and higher education in particular have an obvious effect on the process of budgeting. "Expenditures for higher education have been increasingly carefully scrutinized" as a result of altered public attitudes. These attitudes shifted in the 1970s toward higher education as a personal asset rather than a societal one, and this shift in attitude resulted in a much tighter financial environment. Furthermore, taxpayer revolts have added to pressure for increased institutional accountability (Munitz and Lawless 1986, p. 67).

"Public interest in state finances tends to vary inversely with the state's fiscal condition: When fiscal conditions are poor, the attention level is high, but as conditions improve, other issues generally seem more interesting to those not directly involved in state finances" (Gold 1987, p. 5). During the early to mid-1980s, fiscal conditions in many states were very poor, and public interest was correspondingly high. During this period, "higher education did not fare as well as elementary-secondary (K–12) education in the contest for scarce state budget dollars, but it did benefit from the focus on education" (Gold 1987, p. 17).

Economic conditions and the budget process

Two important economic conditions arising in the 1970s and 1980s were declining economic activity and taxpayer revolts. Each had an effect on the revenues available to states, which in turn affected states' abilities to support higher education. The accompanying shifts in public attitudes interacted with these economic factors.

Michigan is a state where state obligations periodically outstrip available government funds. Such periods have historically been associated with national recessions: Between 1947 and 1972, periods of fiscal crisis followed or accompanied recessions of varying severity. Problems with state revenues in the earlier recessions were met by reluctantly raising taxes until the recession eased and revenues increased. Later recessions, however, brought outright cuts in spending (Brazier 1982). Forecasting revenues is difficult because of economic fluctuations, and expenditures are similarly difficult to predict (Wildavsky 1986).

Tax revolts are epitomized by the passage of Proposition 13 in California in 1978. The large state surplus cushioned the effect for two years, but after 1981 the cushion deflated. Cuts in federal aid and a national recession combined with the effects of the tax cut to erode the state's financial position, interrupting the orderly progress of the budget cycle.

To achieve a formally balanced budget, there has been resort to expedients—one-time ad hoc taxing and spending measures—which provide no lasting basis for sustained financial capacity. . . . The budget is made and remade throughout the fiscal year in a desperate game of catch up to make figures come out even at the end (Caiden and Chapman 1982, p. 118).

A direct effect of revenue constraints on higher education is the increase in tuition rates charged by public institutions. In some states, the legislative appropriation includes tuition and fee revenues, while in others it is treated as institutional revenue or local funds (Mingle 1988). The amount of tuition and fees, it can be argued, is associated with the amount of state appropriations. For example, in the state of Washington, in 1981 to 1983, tuition and fees at public institutions rose from 35 to 79 percent above base levels, in large part as a result of a statewide economic tailspin (Gilmour and Suttle 1984). As part of its "Margin for Excellence" program, the Massachusetts Board of Regents permitted institutions to retain increases in tuition. The new policy, however, is subject to legislative approval and regulations developed by the chancellor (Massachusetts Board of Regents 1988). Thus, both the amount of tuition that can be charged and the use of the revenue is subject to varying state control through the budgetary process.

The politics of the budget process

Five changes in state politics are particularly relevant in discussions of state higher education budget processes: scarcer state resources, more responsibilities for state government, less supportive citizens, increased use of referenda to make major policy decisions, and more complex technology available to interest groups and campaigns. Some of them, notably those directly affecting the availability of resources, have been dealt with by cutting spending, shifting costs, fighting for an increased share of a diminishing budget, and other approaches to managing resources. Another approach attempts to increase state revenues and ultimately the total state budget as well as endeavoring to increase higher education's share of the pie (E. Jones 1984).

Increasing professionalism and numbers of policy makers and staffs in states are modern phenomena. In 1971, for example, 34 of the 148 members of the Michigan legislature had only a high school education. By 1989, just 10 members listed high school as their highest education level. At the upper end of the education scale, those with graduate or professional degrees, the change is also dramatic: By 1989, 68 members held such degrees, compared with 43 in 1971 (Michigan Dept. of State 1971, 1989). The effect of this kind of change within legislatures is felt primarily in the process of gathering information. Staff members lay out options for guiding legislative action, and in the process, they can develop considerable influence. In New York, for example, two committee staff members had no power of their own but were able to pass "virtually final judgment on perhaps 80 percent of Governor Carey's budget requests" through their advice to the leaders of the legislature (Dionne 1979).

The political environment also frequently puts pressure on state decision makers to improve their budgeting. Various budgeting techniques, including formula budgeting, program planning and budgeting systems, zero-base budgeting, and the current interest in budgeting for quality outcomes, are, at least in part, results of political pressures. PPBS and ZBB have both largely become obsolete as approaches to budgeting because of the large amount of time required to implement and use them, but, interestingly, "the economic conditions and political climate of the past few years may be more hospitable to rational decision criteria than the circumstances of the 1960s and 1970s when PPBS and ZBB were introduced" (Abney and Lauth 1986, p. 108). In those years, favorable economic conditions supported incremental decision making, characterized by distributive policies of pluralist politics rather than rational criteria.

Incentives for enhancing quality in higher education are a current approach used in a number of states, though the focus of such efforts has shifted. During the 1980s, some states intensified efforts to improve quality by associating financing with performance objectives or measures of quality (Berdahl

and Studds 1989). States until recently tended to view the quality of programs as dependent on inputs, such as student and faculty characteristics. The 1960 California *Master Plan for Higher Education,* which became a model for statewide higher education planning in the 1960s, included direct statements to this effect. More recently, however, many states have begun expanding their traditional perspective to include issues of educational process as well as inputs (Green 1986). Some states, notably Tennessee, have actively tried to measure outcomes of education at specific institutions. Some institutions are notable in their efforts to measure outcomes like the "value" added to each particular student as a consequence of attending that institution. These approaches represent a market strategy of producing a "product" that is desirable to those outside higher education.

"College presidents have *not* been in the forefront in calling for incentives or greater use of market strategies; those pressures have come from businessmen and state and national political leaders" (Folger 1989, p. 2). In fact, administrators tend to dislike such approaches because their preference is for predictability and stability in budgeting. Using incentives or sanctions tends to destabilize the budget process. The record of these performance incentives is mixed, however, as is their acceptance. State government officials believe that performance funding has become an integral part of the budget process. Performance funding increases officials' willingness to fund higher education. Such programs, however, had little effect on faculty involvement (Folger 1989).

The recent phenomenon of emphasizing quality outputs from higher education is a shift from the traditional emphasis on inputs and administrative process. The shift is one from values of pluralist politics and incrementalism to rational decision making. Data, however, do not indicate that information about effectiveness and efficiency (outputs) was used to a large extent in budget decision making in states. Yet such considerations are not totally ignored (Abney and Lauth 1986).

The State Organizational Filter

The state organizational filter, the set of factors that "modifies" the effect of the external environment on the state higher education budget outcome, consists of the major actors in the process, the timing of the process, and techniques for allocating resources.

Organizational participants in state budgeting

Legislatures have been asserting themselves more strongly, and many have developed strong professional staffs to assist them. Further, the state-level higher education agency has also become more important to the budget process over time. The way the roles are played differs from state to state, however. For example, the level of detailed control over appropriations includes several models (Allen 1980). At the time of the study, 13 states made lump-sum grants to individual institutions, and 11 gave funds to a postsecondary agency or system office. "All of those arrangements give substantial flexibility to institutions within the confines of the political situation and limited direct legislative mandates" (p. 26).

The major actors in the budgeting process are the governor, the higher education community, and the legislature. The higher education community is comprised of the state higher education agency (if any), the governing boards, and the institutions. State higher education agencies may be more closely allied with the executive or with the institutions, while in some states they might take a middle ground among all three of the other major actors. Some observers argue that agency officials (that is, institutions and/or state higher education agencies) are generally seen "as being much more concerned with agency survival and program expansion than with effectiveness and efficiency" (Abney and Lauth 1986, p. 126). These officials are pressured to think this way by constraints from the political environment but also because their jobs are to meet the needs of their clients (students). The governor represents the entire state and must make allocations among competing interests, including those represented by the institutions and agencies (Abney and Lauth 1986).

Process and timing

The timing of budgeting is changing. Where once budgets were written and enacted in a more or less regular cycle, it is less and less the case. Legislatures meet with greater frequency, economic conditions are shifting, and demands for state dollars have increased in number and intensity, necessitating more frequent budgeting. Annual budgeting is declining in use (and presumably in those states with biennial budgets, so too is biennial budgeting). Particularly as economic, social, and political conditions shift, state budgeteers must alter the budget in midyear (Wildavsky 1986).

State governments and higher education institutions operate with differing time frame. A typical politician focuses on the shortest time frame: year to year and election to election. A state budget officer might focus on the budget on which he or she is working at the moment, with an eye to the previous one for comparisons and perhaps to the next one. Institutional officials must have a longer time frame for operations. Not only must they operate from year to year within resources granted by the states and with incoming tuition revenues, but they must also manage commitments that last three, four, five, or more years. Research grants, construction projects, and academic program planning require a perspective extending well beyond the election-to-election focus of politicians. Difficulty arises when elected officials expect a quick solution to long-term, complex problems. The politician might provide funding for one or two years, see little or no result, and threaten to cut off funds. Institutional officials might vigorously implement the program, attempt to modify the proposal for the quick fix to accommodate the need for a longer time frame, or simply accept the money and hope the program will work despite their doubts.

The funding relationship between state and institution: Techniques for allocation

The process of allocating funds, of course, differs from state to state. Fourteen states use some type of formula to allocate funds among institutions, and an additional 15 states use formulas as part of the budget development (request) process (Maryland Higher Education Commission 1988). States using formulas typically have more than one formula to allocate funds to the different functional areas (instruction, research, public service, academic support, student services, institutional support, operations and maintenance/plant, and student aid). A base factor, such as FTE enrollments, staff positions, or square footage is used within the formula to allocate funding, depending on the purpose of the formula.

The trend among states using formulas has been to develop even more complex funding formulas. For example, Mississippi's formula provides funding for eight separate budget categories, resulting from a revision of the process in 1987. Oregon has a separate formula to fund increases in enrollment before appropriations are made. After approval of appropriations, the state uses an allocation model incorporating faculty productivity ratios that are based on peer comparisons with other states in the instruction formula (Maryland Higher Education Commission 1988).

Despite increasingly sophisticated funding formulas, however, concern remains as to the ability of formulas to adequately meet the special needs of different institutions within a state (McKeown 1986). Much literature describes the use of funding formulas for higher education, but little empirical evidence exists as to the overall effectiveness of these formulas in meeting objectives for funding.

Techniques of allocation can also differ within a state. In Michigan, for example, funding for community colleges is allocated on the basis of a formula, while funding for the state universities is not. The process for decision making differs in many ways, but, most important, it differs in the timing of attention to the bottom line. Based on one author's observation as a legislative staff person, it was apparent that in the appropriations for community colleges, legislators first review the segments of the formula and then look at their impact on total spending for each college. In the process for state universities, the discussions tend to focus first on the bottom line and only secondarily on the means of building to that level.

Techniques of allocating funds, especially funding formulas, can also vary depending on the portion of the process they address. In Florida, for example, one formula is used for acquiring resources and another for allocating them. Arizona, Kansas, and Texas use formulas to fund only enrollment growth (Maryland Higher Education Commission 1988). Different actors in the process may use different techniques of allocation as well: The state legislature might not use a formula, but a coordinating agency might use one (Allen 1980).

Summary

Most of the literature on budgeting focuses on the inputs and outputs of budgeting for higher education. Little of it captures the process itself with all its complexities. More research on state budgeting processes for higher education is needed. From what we know, it is evident that funding for higher education must compete for diminishing state resources. State officials are becoming more sophisticated in their knowledge about higher education. They may be less in awe of the academy and more willing to ask questions about its value. The

Difficulty arises when elected officials expect a quick solution to long-term, complex problems.

general public is also less in awe of higher education, and it too is asking questions about its value. Public attitudes about higher education have shifted from value to society to value to the individual.

Budgeting is buffeted by fiscal constraints, and, as a result, it is a process that occurs with more frequency and less stability. Tax revolts and general economic malaise take their toll on states' abilities to pass and maintain a budget for an entire year.

Techniques of allocation vary among states. Several states use funding formulas for at least part of the higher education budget. Those states that use formulas to fund higher education have been adding even greater complexity to the formulas in recent years. Despite this increased sophistication, however, the differentiation or lack or differentiation between higher education institutions in a state remains a perennial concern with regard to funding formulas.

BUDGETARY OUTCOMES

The state budget document is more than a book of numbers and rhetoric. In the larger context of state government and politics, the budget may be seen as a unique product shaped by a unique environment interacting with a dynamic process. The budget reflects the "state of the state" as well as sets forth the major policy preferences of state government within those external constraints. "If politics is regarded as conflict over whose preferences are to prevail in the determination of policy, then the budget records the outcomes of this struggle" (Wildavsky 1986, p. 9).

Higher education, although it performs a valued function in the state, is not immune from the political economy of the state budget process. Only a finite amount of state revenues can be distributed among state services, and higher education is subject to the same environmental forces and dynamic processes as other state services. Moreover, the state higher education budget sets forth the major state policy preferences for higher education. This section analyzes the budget as the state's primary policy document on higher education and budgeting as the process for bringing these policy concerns to fruition. The areas discussed include accountability, costs, productivity, and quality (including fiscal incentives), affordability, economic development, minority and nontraditional students, and independent higher education. Although some of these areas may not be directly identified as budget items per se, all have budgetary implications for higher education.

Accountability

A term used often with respect to higher education in recent years is "accountability." Only recently, however, has accountability been tied directly to the budget process. The advent of fiscal incentive programs, for example, represents an attempt by policy makers to tie funding to specific outcomes. "The utility of the budget as a device for accountability . . . depends heavily on the extent to which it reflects state priorities and ties this funding to performance" (D. Jones 1984, p. 16).

Generally, the external assessment of higher education's "performance" has been less than congratulatory.

Other public perceptions suggest that there is waste and duplication in . . . higher education, that faculty do not spend enough time on instruction, that minority student access and retention rates are too low, and that the price of education has increased at too great a rate. Whether entirely accurate or not, these perceptions represent concerns about the quality, cost-effectiveness, and accountability of . . . higher education (Committee on Scope 1990, p. 1).

Dealing with accountability can occur at the beginning as well as at the end of the budgetary process. This discussion of accountability begins with a conceptual analysis, followed by a description of accountability mechanisms.

The concept of accountability

Although the word is much used by state policy makers and in higher education circles, an exact definition of accountability remains elusive. Accountability is hard to define because the term refers to a process rather than a product (Hartmark 1978). Accountability has also been viewed as a means as opposed to an end in achieving greater efficiency and administrative control in higher education (Hines 1988a). Further, between the 1960s and 1980s, the focus of accountability evolved from a fiduciary orientation to an orientation focused on outcome (Mingle and Lenth 1989). In essence, the concept of accountability refers to the responsibility of higher education to report on its failures and achievements to state government.

The current view of accountability is as a concept having several dimensions occurring within different policy domains:

1. *Systemic accountability:* dealing with the fundamental purposes of higher education;
2. *Substantive accountability:* dealing with the values and norms within higher education;
3. *Programmatic accountability:* dealing with academic and other programs;
4. *Procedural accountability:* dealing with institutional and administrative procedures;
5. *Fiduciary accountability:* dealing with the finance of higher education (Hartmark and Hines 1986).

"With each of these dimensions (although the concern here is with fiduciary accountability), it is important to remember that accountability has always involved process and product, but until recently the focus was on process and not product."*

---

*E.R. Hines, June 26, 1990, personal communication.

In short, in regard to state budgeting for higher education, the concept of accountability has traditionally focused on *how and why* higher education spends state funds as opposed to the *result* of those expenditures.

Systems for implementing accountability mechanisms
Because the emphasis in accountability has traditionally been primarily procedural, the discussion about this concept has evolved largely around the systems that have been devised to ensure accountability. Three widely used accountability mechanisms include the performance audit, program review, and assessment, all of which have similar elements. A performance audit is "an assessment of how effectively an activity or organization achieves its goals and objectives. It is a natural extension of fiscal and management audits going beyond relatively narrow questions of how funds are used to questions about effectiveness" (Floyd 1982, p. 33). Performance audits typically are conducted by commissions established by the executive or legislative branch. While the merits of performance audits are unclear, observers have pointed out numerous problems. Some functional limitations include the lack of appropriate performance indicators and the failure to establish clear standards and processes before the audit (Floyd 1982). Performance audits have several limitations:

1. They tend to ignore the broader context in which higher education exists;
2. They focus on the structure of the state higher education agency rather than on the effectiveness of planning, evaluation, and allocating resources within the system;
3. Auditors are often inexperienced and unqualified to make judgments about issues in higher education; and
4. The inherent political dimension of performance audits may bias the outcome of the audit (Folger and Berdahl 1988).

Program review is "an assessment of the need for and effectiveness of a proposed or existing program" (Floyd 1982, p. 26). The responsibility for academic program review lies primarily within the state higher education board or agency, although campus representatives and outside consultants are often used in the process. The purposes of program review are assessing the program's productivity and effectiveness,

suggesting ways to improve quality, ensuring efficient use of resources, including reducing unnecessary duplication of programs across campuses, aiding planning, and satisfying the statutory requirements of the state higher education agency (Conrad and Wilson 1985; Wallhaus 1982). Current models in place for reviewing academic programs include (1) the *goal-based model*, in which program goals are identified and data are generated to evaluate the degree of fit between the goals and the current status of the program; (2) the *decision-making model*, in which information is generated to examine such areas as context, input, process, and product; and (3) *connoisseurship*, in which external experts critically evaluate a program (Conrad and Wilson 1985). The effectiveness of program review rests largely on the ability of the state higher education agency and the campus to come to an agreement about the purposes and possible outcomes of the program review before initiating the review process (Hines 1988a).

Assessment includes many of the elements contained within the performance audit and the program review, and it shares the same ultimate goal of improving quality. The primary difference of assessment is that it focuses on the evaluation of student outcomes in higher education. Another difference is that while the burden of the performance audit and the program review rests primarily on the state agency, assessment refocuses "institutional responsibility on the process and effectiveness of student learning" (Mingle and Lenth 1989, p. 9). Assessment comes in several different forms. The most obvious are the statewide student tests used in Florida and Texas and institutionally based tests like the "value-added" assessment at Northeast Missouri State University. Nontest assessment methods are also currently in place, such as the monitoring of academic programs and the monitoring of students' learning and growth (Hines 1988a). The benefits of effective assessment are the improvement of teaching and learning, feedback that could improve academic programs, and enhancement of higher education's credibility with the wider public (E.F. Carlisle 1988). The potential drawbacks of an assessment program are in measuring that which is not meant to be measured or, conversely, not measuring what is meant to be measured.

The critical question about assessment is the purpose of the assessment. Even more important is the answer.

That . . . a state must or wishes to assess its students . . . is not a sufficient answer. Several reasons have been proposed—among them program improvement, individual student learning, accountability, budgeting, and placement. To some extent, each requires a different form or means of assessment. . . . Purpose not only influences the means; it also determines the locus for assessment. Depending on the objective the appropriate place or level may be institutional, departmental, or individual . . . for without a clear sense of purpose, it will be impossible to choose meaningfully what and how to assess (E.F. Carlisle 1988, p. 4).

In essence, effective assessment requires a clear sense of what is to be measured and why. Further, it requires a commitment from all parties involved as to what is to be measured and why.

The new accountability and state funding for higher education

The major similarity of all three of these accountability mechanisms is in the collection of volumes of data to support the processes. At the state level, a great deal of time and energy go into collecting data from institutions through a variety of surveys and other instruments and then sending them to the federal government and/or other agencies concerned with higher education. As a consequence, whether by choice or lack of time or other resources, the focus in the past has been on the *process* of reporting data as opposed to the critical analysis of what the data mean for the purpose of change (that is, the *product),* and it has two negative implications for current accountability measures. First, "state boards [that] assume this data collection responsibility become, in a political sense, responsible for the performance of institutions. Institutions, on the other hand, can become curiously relieved of the responsibility to change" (Mingle and Lenth 1989, p. 3). Instead of shared responsibility in the accountability process, the state agency is perceived as the dominant party in this relationship. As a result, the second implication is one of increased tension along the accountability/autonomy axis (shown earlier in figure 2). The state is seen as further intruding into the jurisdiction of the academy, which in turn undermines the purpose of accountability mechanisms. The ultimate result is that policy makers' and the public's desire for accountability goes unmet.

As higher education moves into the 1990s, it is evident that it will be necessary for higher education to improve upon the way it demonstrates its accountability to the state. The establishment of a new accountability structure begins with a reexamination of the goals and objectives for higher education (Mingle and Lenth 1989). The establishment of goals and objectives for higher education is by definition a process of consensus building among the primary constituencies: policy makers, administrators, faculty, students, and the public. In the future, accountability will still involve the collection of data, but the purpose for the collection of data will parallel the goals and objectives for higher education, thus reducing the tension between campus and state. The focus is on the feedback provided by the data regarding progress toward the established goals and objectives and not on the reporting of the data. "New systems of accountability are becoming fundamentally 'change instruments' not reporting mechanisms . . . . The primary accountability mechanisms are agenda setting (and the related policy analyses and data collections) and funding mechanisms" (Mingle and Lenth 1989, p. 4). Accountability systems of the future will increasingly be placed at various stages of the budget process. These systems will be used to determine both the efficiency and adequacy of state funding for higher education as well as the effectiveness of the state and institutions in meeting stated goals through this funding.

Costs, Productivity, and Quality

Like accountability, "costs" (institutional), "productivity," and "quality" are increasingly being used together in higher education circles. These three words have become almost a litany recited by state policy makers to the leaders of the higher education community: Costs should be kept down and productivity increased while maintaining (or improving) quality in higher education. This subsection outlines what these concepts mean, their interrelationships, and their implications for the budget.

Costs

The word "cost" is usually thought of in terms of what we spend to acquire some good or service. Higher education costs are "the expenditure by a college [or] university to acquire the services of land, labor, or capital, to purchase goods and services, or to provide student financial aid. . . . More accurately and fundamentally, 'cost' refers to the opportunities sacrificed by reason of such expenditures" (Bowen 1980, p. xx). According to this definition then, higher education incurs costs in two senses: once for the item it bought (its monetary cost) and once for the item it could not buy because of the one it did (the opportunity cost). Opportunity costs are inherent in any budgetary decision, given limited resources and seemingly unlimited demands.

The costs of higher education follow certain "natural" laws:

1. *The dominant goals of institutions are educational excellence, prestige, and influence; . . . .*
2. *In quest of excellence, prestige, and influence, there is virtually no limit to the amount of money an institution could spend for seemingly fruitful educational ends; . . . .*
3. *Each institution raises all the money it can; . . . .*
4. *Each institution spends all it raises; . . . .*
5. *The cumulative effect of the preceding four laws is toward ever-increasing expenditure* (Bowen 1980, pp. 19–20).

In part, these "laws" are a function of the not-for-profit status of higher education institutions. In colleges and universities as well as other not-for-profit organizations, no real pressure exists to keep costs low, given that their single purpose is to provide the best possible service to the clientele. "Additional income ('profits') is used to expand existing programs and to establish new ones, with a reluctance to reallocate resources by eliminating or pruning programs that are perceived as less productive" (Levin 1989, p. 1).

The cumulative effect of these laws has been clearly evident in recent years. Inflation in the costs of higher education (as measured by the Higher Education Price Index [HEPI]) rose at the same rate as inflation in the general economy (as measured by the Consumer Price Index [CPI]) until the early 1980s. Throughout the 1980s, however, inflation in higher education costs grew by 4 to 10 percent annually, compared to 2 to 4 percent annual inflation in the general economy (Halstead 1989a). And this inflation occurred during a time when state support for higher education (especially public higher education) was stagnating or declining in many states (Hines, Hickrod, and Pruyne 1989). The result of this decline in state funding led many institutions to raise tuition by double-digit percentages to make up the funding (Halstead 1989a), again illustrating the "natural law" of higher education, which holds that colleges and universities will not sacrifice institutional integrity and quality simply because of fiscal exigencies.

Costs in higher education have been increasing at such a rapid rate for three reasons: "cost disease," the "growth force," and "organizational slack" (Massy 1989). "Cost disease" refers to the fact that higher education is highly labor intensive, and because of it, higher education and other "nonprogressive industries" do not benefit from the adoption of labor-saving technologies to reduce costs. Other "progressive industries," however, will be able to benefit from these technologies, resulting in increased productivity and in turn increased wages in that sector. Because higher education and other nonprogressive industries must compete with progressive industries in acquiring labor, these increased labor costs will be transferred to the nonprogressive sector. Thus, assuming the productivity of higher education remains constant, costs of higher education will grow at about the same rate as the general increase in productivity in the economy, which is slightly above the rate of inflation. "Growth force" refers to the fact that in their desire to improve or maintain quality, colleges and universities add new programs and services while maintaining all existing programs and services. Thus, institutions are consistently in a net growth mode. And "organizational slack" refers to the simple waste and inefficiency that occur in all organizations. Resources are not being used to their greatest potential. When slack remains within an organization, as it often does within colleges and universities, additional costs are incurred to deal with the problems caused by the slack.

Productivity

Closely related to costs of higher education is the concept of productivity. In simple terms, productivity refers to the ratio of outputs to inputs, where higher ratios reflect greater "productivity" and vice versa. In industrial settings, productivity is relatively easy to measure. One would need only to take the total product (output) of a company and divide the input of choice: per worker, per dollar spent, and so on. Measuring productivity in higher education is a much messier proposition. In higher education, although inputs are relatively easy to identify (that is land, labor, and capital costs), "outcomes are diffuse and difficult to measure" (Mingle and Lenth 1989, p. 13).

For many years, especially in states where formula funding was used to finance higher education, productivity in higher education was seen in terms of enrollments. Institutions that were able to increase their enrollments were the beneficiaries of increased funding through the formula (Leslie and Ramey 1986), and much of it had to do with the meritocratic goal of state and federal governments in maintaining access to higher education for all eligible citizens. Institutions that increased their enrollments were seen as meeting that goal and were rewarded as such. In recent years, however, much has been said of the declining productivity of American higher education. Part of this debate hinges on the seemingly unending dilemma surrounding the measurement of higher education's productivity. Steeply rising costs combined with the trend toward an orientation focused on outcomes in higher education have led many state policy makers to question the results of public expenditures. Increased enrollments are no longer automatically assumed to be desirable ends and thus are no longer rewarded with increased funding. In fact, increased enrollments sometimes result in decreased funding for higher education (Leslie and Ramey 1986). Further, state-level efforts to assess outcomes of higher education are often seen as ineffective or intrusive.

A somewhat broader dimension of the issue of productivity in higher education is the extent to which higher education is perceived as improving the productivity of the state and national economies. Conceptually, higher education and state/ national economic productivity are now seen as being inextricably linked (E.R. Carlisle 1988). Higher education produces both a more educated work force and research activities that improve the productivity and competitiveness of the economy. A recent meta-analysis of the economic value of higher education found that, "overall, education may contribute to as much as 50 percent or more of growth in the economy and higher education may contribute almost half of this [amount]" (Leslie and Brinkman 1988, p. 82). As a result, the question remains as to what extent ambiguities in the measurement

For policy makers, "quality" . . . has become a political maypole around which few can afford not to dance.

of higher education's productivity have a negative effect on the productivity of state and national economies.

Quality

Even more ambiguous than the definition and measurement of higher education's productivity is that of the quality of higher education. These ambiguities aside, the quality movement in higher education includes some central tenets:

1. College students should take, and faculty should teach, college-level courses; remediation detracts from the quality of the institution.
2. The public sector should be stratified; the integrity of the "flagship" must be maintained through toughened admissions standards, even at the expense of "lesser" institutions.
3. Institutions should serve the cause of economic development; a "quality" institution is a big draw in economic development (Mingle 1989).

For policy makers, "quality" higher education has become a political maypole around which few can afford not to dance.

At the same time, institutions have begun to come to terms with this political meaning of quality, and their leaders have started to work these concepts into their own rhetoric. Quality to any institution of higher education depends heavily on the acquisition of resources. In fact, quality in public universities—as measured by faculty productivity, student competition, and so on—is significantly correlated with the amount of state support for higher education (Volkwein 1989). Effective institutions "interact with their environments in ways that enhance the acquisition of resources" (p. 149). It would appear then that those institutions that most effectively articulate state goals for the enhancement of "quality" will be the ones to get the lion's share of higher education appropriations, which in turn reinforces the quality of the institution. For colleges and universities, then, enhancing quality (or the acquisition of additional resources) has become heavily dependent on the ability to speak the same language as state policy makers.

Budgetary implications of cost, productivity, and quality

The interrelationships among cost, productivity, and quality are relatively clear, but the achievement of desired budgetary ends related to these concepts is less than clear. "When external constituents complain about the high costs of higher education or its lack of productivity, they seldom wish to see societal commitment reduced in absolute terms" (Mingle and Lenth 1989, p. 14). It is evident, however, that state budgeting for higher education will need to change to address increased costs, lagging productivity, and the need to enhance quality. Researchers and policy makers alike increasingly cite three steps: (1) becoming more goal driven, (2) using constraints on resources, and (3) making better use of incentives.

Becoming more goal driven. One proposed system for improving on these areas in higher education consists of goals, incentives, and information (Levin 1989). Goals provide the cornerstones for reducing costs, improving productivity, and enhancing quality. By establishing clear goals and priorities, an institution has a blueprint upon which it can effectively maximize the use of its limited resources to achieve these goals and priorities. By the same token, if an institution does not possess a clear sense of its "mission," resources are squandered. Of course, the establishment of goals will not necessarily ensure that individuals within the institution will pursue them. Incentives are needed to encourage individuals within the institution to align themselves with the institution's mission to reach those goals. Such incentives may be related to salary, not related to salary and extrinsic (awards, travel funds, personal computers, for example), or intrinsic (greater autonomy, more challenging assignments, and so on). For an institution, an important incentive might be the ability to retain savings from reduced costs and improved productivity. Finally, information systems are needed to provide feedback to the institution and the state as to whether or not the institution is achieving its goals (accountability) and whether better alternatives are available to meet the desired outcomes. Information on alternatives is one of the least developed areas within the topic of costs, productivity, and quality (Levin 1989).

Using constraints on resources. A somewhat different system for reducing costs, improving productivity, and enhancing quality consists of resource constraints, strategic thinking, incentives, and individual and group empowerment (Massy 1989). Resource constraints include the end of "cost-plus"

pricing in higher education, which has contributed to the large increases in tuition and fees in all sectors of higher education. Resource constraints force the institution to consider which areas could be reallocated to other parts of the organization and, ultimately, to the institution's goals and priorities. This process results in strategic thinking regarding the institution's purpose and direction and ultimately use and allocation of resources within the institution. Should the institution continue to pursue a full range of academic programs at all levels, or should it consider concentrating its resources at the undergraduate level and improving the quality of the undergraduate curriculum? Incentives, rewards, and recognition provide for positive reinforcement of activities that further the institution's goals and identify negative behaviors. Related is the empowerment of individuals to ensure that the necessary work gets done. For workers in knowledge, such as those in higher education, autonomy is a powerful incentive in the performance of one's job. Similarly, the lack of autonomy tends to stifle creativity and ultimately work against the goals of reducing costs, improving productivity, and enhancing quality.

Making better use of incentives. In recent years, an area related to costs, productivity, and quality in which some states have been extremely active has been the area of fiscal incentives. In essence, the entire budget may be seen as one big fiscal incentive for higher education.

> *The budget is one of the two primary mechanisms available to state government for signaling its priorities and for translating plans into action. . . . As the major funder of public institutions of postsecondary education, state government has available to it, through the budget process, a potentially very long lever to be used in bringing about desired change* (Jones 1989, p. 1).

During the 1980s, however, many state higher education leaders intensified efforts to improve quality through the use of competitive, categorical, and incentive financial strategies (Berdahl and Studds 1989). Though base budgets remain the main source of funding for higher education, these incentive programs have become a way for policy makers to place their policy goals for higher education in the spotlight and to reward those who further these goals. Some in higher education view these programs not as incentives but as threats to the base budget.

Three states that are substantially involved in incentive funding programs are Florida, Tennessee, and Ohio. Florida has a number of fiscal incentive programs, including Centers of Excellence, Eminent Scholars, and an Equipment Trust Fund. Between fiscal years 1974 and 1989, the state put $115.7 million into the categorical programs, $54.2 million through incentive grants for its senior institutions, and $10.3 million into its competitive programs (Berdahl and Studds 1989). Tennessee has had in place for over 11 years a funding mechanism that ties improvements in undergraduate education at state universities, community colleges, and technical institutes with additional unrestricted funding. During this period, over $102 million was allocated through this program (Folger 1989). Ohio's Selective Excellence Program is actually a collection of seven incentive programs, the first two of which (Eminent Scholars and Program Excellence) were established in 1983 (Hairston 1989). Between 1983 and 1989, the state invested a total of $157.6 million in this program (Ohio Board of Regents 1989). The goals of these programs range from improving undergraduate education in all sectors of higher education to expanding research. The empirical evidence on the overall effectiveness of these or similar programs in meeting state goals is limited and inconclusive, however (Levin 1989).

In summary, the evidence on the budgetary implications of costs, productivity, and quality suggests five imperatives for the future. First, in dealing with these dilemmas, state and institutional higher education leaders must clearly agree on what the policy goals for higher education are or ought to be at all levels. Second, state policy makers must commit themselves to constraints on resources and enforce them firmly. Third, institutional leaders must take a hard look at options for reallocation for their institutions. Fourth, state policy makers may have to allow budgeting to become more decentralized to allow more flexibility on campus in the pursuit of these goals. And fifth, all participants within the state higher education budget process should encourage a certain degree of experimentation, some risk taking, and, above all, innovation within the educational enterprise (Levin 1989).

Affordability

During the 1980s, the affordability of higher education began to develop as a significant issue for state policy makers. Between fiscal years 1981 and 1988, average tuition at public institutions increased by 83 percent and average tuition at private institutions grew by 95 percent, while the CPI and median family income grew by 34 percent and 50 percent, respectively (Halstead 1989a). Further, increased inequality in income among American families has led to a vanishing middle class and a nation of haves and have nots resulting from the growing income gap between individuals with high school and college diplomas (Levy 1989). The traditional policy levers available to state higher education policy makers for dealing with the question of affordability include setting public tuition levels and providing student financial aid. In recent years, an additional lever has been state mechanisms to help parents save for children's college education, such as tuition prepayment and savings plans.

Tuition policy

Traditionally, tuition in the public sector has been seen as a way to plug the gap between state appropriations and expected expenditures for the coming fiscal year, leading to an inverse relationship between the two sources of funds. During the 1980s, the rapid rise in institutional costs and expenditures, coupled with a decline in state appropriations, led to the substantial growth in tuition at public institutions (Wittstruck and Bragg 1988). Further, empirical evidence suggests that increases in tuition adversely affect enrollments (approximately 1.8 to 2.4 percent decline for every $100 increase in price) (Leslie and Brinkman 1988). An added complication has been the increased focus on the quality of higher education in the midst of the rising costs of attendance. "Nobody likes higher prices; that's a given. But if higher prices are linked to lower quality, the result can be devastating" (Rosensweig 1990, p. 44).

In an effort to address the issue of affordability, several states have reexamined or are in the process of reexamining their policies for setting tuition. A survey by the State Higher Education Executive Officers (SHEEOs) indicates that eight states have statutes that set expected tuition revenue as a specified percentage of instructional costs or state appropriations and that four states establish tuition and fee rates through statute or rules as a specified percentage of cost per student or state appropriations (Mingle 1988). Further, the survey indicates that over half of the states in the country use the CPI or HEPI, either formally or informally, in setting tuition, which indicates that states are trying to minimize the traditional role of public tuition as a plug by linking it to external factors. The effect of these efforts has not yet displaced the traditional inverse relationship between tuition and state appropriations for higher education, however (Hauptman 1989).

Although state policy makers have no direct influence over setting tuition in the private sector, some states have attempted to indirectly influence the growth in tuition at private institutions through direct institutional grant programs. These programs are usually based on the number of residents enrolled, the number of degrees conferred by the institution, or contracts for specific programs (Lapovsky and Allard 1986). As tuition and fees remain the largest source of revenue for private institutions, any additional outside funding could help preclude the need to raise tuition in the private sector.

Student financial aid

A related policy lever addressing the issue of affordability is state-funded, need-based grant and scholarship programs. Student aid has been shown to increase access to higher education, promote choice, and improve persistence among recipients (Leslie and Brinkman 1988). Every state has some form of need-based student aid program for undergraduate students. In fiscal year 1988, states awarded $1.8 billion in grant aid to 1.7 million students (Reeher and Davis 1988). The requirements for and eligibility of students to participate vary from state to state. Although it is acknowledged that the amount spent by states on student financial aid pales in comparison with that spent by the federal government, it remains an important policy lever.

In the past, the arguments about affordability, tuition, and student financial aid have tended to be either for low or no tuition/low financial aid or for high tuition/high financial aid (Wittstruck and Bragg 1988). The argument for low or no tuition assumes that society is the ultimate beneficiary of an educated population; thus, government should subsidize all or a significant portion of the operating costs of higher education institutions. Conversely, the position for high tuition/high student aid argues that in general the individual, not society, is the primary beneficiary of a higher education and that those who can afford it should pay full price, allowing the government to concentrate on subsidizing needy individuals through student aid. Virtually all states identified as having high tuition also have large student aid programs (Mullen 1988).

In recent years, state support for student aid programs has dwindled along with state general appropriations for higher education, while tuition has increased. Nationally, need-based grants kept pace with tuition in only about one-third of the states between 1983 and 1988 (Halstead 1989a; Reeher and Davis 1988). Federal grant programs, especially the Pell grant program, did not keep pace with tuition during the 1980s (Hansen 1989). It would seem that tuition, financial aid, and institutional support would be linked at the state level to meet the objectives of student aid policies, regardless of the underlying philosophy within the state. A recent survey revealed, however, that only 17 SHEEOs felt that these policies were closely linked within their states (Curry 1988). Thus, the real policy issue is not whether or not state government should provide student subsidies for higher education, for both high- and low-tuition states provide subsidies in one way or another. Instead, the real issue lies in the development of a cohesive plan ensuring that policies for tuition, student aid, and institutional support are linked in a way that is adequate to finance the costs of higher education.

State tuition prepayment and savings plans

Initial state involvement in tuition prepayment and savings plans developed during the 1986 and 1987 legislative sessions (McGuinness and Paulson 1989). Michigan was the first state to enact a prepayment plan (the Michigan Education Trust) in 1986. In 1987, Illinois created and enacted the Illinois College Savings Bond Program. As of September 1989, 11 states had tuition prepayment plans, and 19 states had college savings bond programs. Of those programs enacted, three states have implemented tuition prepayment plans, and 12 states have conducted at least one college savings bond sale (McGuinness and Paulson 1989).

Tuition prepayment plans allow parents to prepay tuition at current or discounted rates at state institutions of higher education several years in advance of their child's entry. In Florida, parents may also prepay room and board at any state university. In return for the prepayment, the state guarantees that tuition will be covered in full by the plan at the time of matriculation. The potential benefits of these plans for participants are obvious, given the rapid growth in tuition and fees during the 1980s. The plans also have a number of potential drawbacks for state policy makers, however: the inability of legislatures or institutions to raise tuition in the future because of the plan's considerations, the risk that growth in the plan's assets will not keep pace with growth in tuition, and the fact that those who can afford to participate in the plan may not really need to, while those who could most benefit from such a plan (that is, low- and middle-income families) will probably not be able to afford to participate (Layzell 1988a). Other disadvantages include the lack of flexibility these plans provide and the fact that they might promote unfair competitive advantages between certain types of institutions (Anderson 1988a).

College savings bond programs are typically structured as part of a state's general obligation bond sale for the year. The bonds are zero-coupon bonds bought at a discount, with the proceeds paid at maturity. They are most often sold with face values of $5,000 and maturities ranging from five to 20 years, with interest rates between 6 and 8 percent (McGuinness and Paulson 1989). Typically, the bonds are exempt from both federal and state taxes. In some states, additional incentives, such as cash bonuses, are in place to influence buyers to use the bonds for college.

Such bonds have several benefits. Their relatively low cost makes them an investment that is available to a broader spectrum of a state's population. Parents are not locked into a certain institution or type of institution. And the state assumes no risk with regard to future tuition rates, given that no promise is made that proceeds of the bonds will keep pace with tuition. Unfortunately, this benefit is also the concept's biggest drawback, as, historically, tax-exempt savings bonds have barely kept up with inflation (Anderson 1988c). As noted previously, tuition outpaced inflation throughout the 1980s. Thus, parents who invest in these bonds may well not be meeting their goal of saving for the future education of their children. Another drawback includes the fact that too much zero-coupon debt could adversely affect the state's future credit rating, given that payment of such debt is shifted to future administrations.

... historically, tax-exempt savings bonds have barely kept up with inflation.

Because tuition prepayment and college saving plans are so new, no empirical evidence exists about their effectiveness in meeting objectives for affordability. While both make political and practical sense to policy makers, if any of the negative arguments presented in either case hold true, the possibility exists that these programs may be doing more to hurt affordability initiatives than to help them. Both alternatives require careful monitoring and gathering of empirical data in the coming years to evaluate their effectiveness fully.

Economic Development

For state policy makers, the potential use of higher education in the state's economic development has become a major issue. For most states, economic development is synonymous with the attraction of high-technology industries, which involves higher education. "Economic planners increasingly regard academic institutions as critical resources in strategies to reinvigorate mature industries and stimulate new, 'sunrise' industries" (Johnson 1984, p. i). Consequently, some states have begun to implement new economic development programs through the budget process for higher education. Interestingly, one study found that states that have promoted themselves as preferential sites for business development also tended to have expanded governmental investment in higher education (Slaughter and Silva 1985). The primary ways that higher education has become involved in economic development have been in the forms of research activities, education and training for the work force, and business partnerships with higher education.

Research activities

Basic research activities are the cornerstone of a nation's economic development, and most basic research is carried on at major research universities. Research is the catalyst for technological innovation, which leads to improved productivity and economic growth (E.R. Carlisle 1988). In the past, the federal government was the primary source of government funding for research, but in recent years, state governments have been taking a larger role in funding research within higher education, either by fully funding research projects or by leveraging funds through challenge grant programs. Ohio implemented its Research Challenge Program in 1985 to stimulate new and expanded research at colleges and universities. It provides a partial match through state funds to research projects with a high probability of securing outside funds. Between 1985 and 1989, the state invested $50.3 million in this program (Ohio Board of Regents 1989). California established the Microelectronics and Computer Research Opportunities Program in 1981 to promote research in microelectronics technology. The program provides matching funds for faculty research projects and provides fellowships to graduate students in the University of California system (Maryland State Board 1986).

Education and training of the work force
An important dual component in attracting and retaining high-technology industries within a state is an educated work force and the ability to provide training to meet high-technology companies' needs for workers. It is even more imperative, given the fact that the gap between the demands for labor of high-technology industries and the current supply of workers qualified to meet this demand nationwide has grown significantly over time (Johnston and Associates 1987). Colleges and universities have been seen as a means to improve the quality of the state's work force as well as to improve ongoing training for the employees of high-technology businesses. Universities provide graduates trained in engineering, science, and math these companies need. The majority of active education and training of the work force is being done by community colleges (Hines 1988a), and community colleges often develop specialized training courses for a company's labor supply. In North Carolina, for example, a representative from the community colleges is sent along on state business-recruiting trips who often guarantees a trained work force on the day the business opens if the company will locate within the state. Even so, some states have lagged in their financial support of community college initiatives, thus weakening an important link (Nazario 1990).

Business partnerships with higher education
The connection between higher education and high-technology industry has three major links: research, human resource development, and technology transfer (Johnson 1984). Technology transfer is probably the most important of the three for retaining and strengthening relationships with companies and ultimately perpetuating economic growth.

Technology transfer involves the commercialization of research results (Johnson 1984). From the business perspective, the successful transfer from laboratory to commercial production is the most important consideration in remaining within a certain location. State initiatives for the transfer of technology include research parks, business incubators, and consulting/extension services (Anderson 1988b).

One of the oldest and best-known examples of partnerships for the purpose of technology transfer is Research Triangle Park in North Carolina. The park, begun in 1956, combines the resources of the state, three universities, private industry, and the federal government in ventures that ensure that technology transfer remains a smooth process. A more recent example is Ohio's Thomas Edison Program, which consists of three components: a seed development fund that matches state funds with private funds in developing new products, technology centers at universities to explore areas of technological concern within the neighboring business community, and incubators to provide academic expertise in setting up new technology-based companies (Maryland State Board 1986).

Some caveats about economic development

Despite all of the potential financial benefits higher education can reap in the state economic development game, a number of caveats remain. First, despite its altruistic motives, economic development remains a political instrument. "Creating jobs, reducing unemployment, . . . and stimulating economic activity offer politicians considerable grist for their mills" (Hines 1988a, p. 63). And depending on the political winds, it could prove to be either a help or a hindrance to a state's higher education leadership. Thus, higher education should be careful about the alliances it forms in the process of participating in a state's economic development efforts. Second, economic development is a long-term proposition, and a quick-fix mentality could cause problems for higher education. Third, the fundamental differences between the academic and the business worlds should never be forgotten. These dissimilarities are found in two sets of different values. With regard to work values, academics find the *means* most important, while businesspeople find the *end product* most important. And with regard to lifestyle, the life of the academic tends to be much more bureaucratic, less stressful, and generally more secure than that of the businessperson (Bird and Allen 1989). If not controlled, these differences could well hamper development activities. And fourth, evaluations of the effectiveness of economic development efforts involving higher education have been sketchy up to now (Anderson 1988b). Thus, state policy makers should be careful about the amount of funding dedicated to such initiatives.

Minority and Nontraditional Students

Two policy issues that have gained importance in the past decade are the issues of minority students' achievement and the accommodation of nontraditional students. These issues have gained significantly in importance at the state level, while, at the same time, higher education has come under fire for failing to meet the needs of these two groups:

> *American colleges and universities have proven more adept at marketing to nontraditional students than at tailoring educational programs to meet their needs, while, ironically, that same marketing has failed to end the persistent underrepresentation of blacks and Hispanics, along with poorer whites and Native-Americans, among college students, staff, and faculty (Policy Perspectives 1990, p. 1).*

These two major trends are causing problems for higher education at a time when higher education is being asked to help with a number of economic and social problems.

Minority students' achievement

The minority population in this country has grown dramatically over the past decade, primarily African-Americans, Hispanics, and Asians. Our population has become more diverse than at any other time in history. The same degree of diversity does not exist in higher education, however. Between 1976 and 1986, the enrollment of African-Americans in higher education declined from 9.4 percent of all enrollments to 8.6 percent of all enrollments, while the Hispanic share increased from 3.5 percent to 5 percent of all enrollments (U.S Dept. of Education 1988, table 146). Although the representation of Hispanic students has increased over time, the fact that, during the 1980s, the Hispanic population grew five times as fast as non-Hispanics and that they currently represent 8 percent of the total population indicates underrepresentation

in higher education *(Business Week* 1989). Interestingly, most institutions realize that they are not improving the achievement of minority students. A recent national survey of campus administrators found that two-thirds rated their institution's performance as "fair" or "poor" in recruiting African-American and Hispanic students. And 40 percent rated efforts to retain African-American and Hispanic students as "fair" or "poor" (El-Khawas 1988).

Because of these factors, state policy makers have started to become involved in initiatives for minority students. Two of the most common programmatic initiatives have been student aid programs for minority students and collaborative efforts within higher education and between higher education and elementary/secondary education related to the progress of minorities (Hines 1988a). An example of the latter is the Minority Educational Achievement grant enabled by the Illinois Higher Education Cooperation Act. The state has allocated a total of $12.5 million for the grant since its inception in fiscal year 1985 to foster cooperative programs among institutions of higher education in Illinois designed to improve the representation of minority students. One specific example of such a cooperative venture being funded through this program is the Chicago Area Health and Medical Careers Program, involving seven area medical schools (public and private), one university, and two not-for-profit organizations. The objective of this program is to increase the number of African-American and Hispanic physicians and other health professionals. Students are recruited from the sixth grade through college for participation in a structured multiyear program providing academic support, guidance counseling, interactions with role models in the health professions, and numerous attempts at intervention.

Nontraditional students

Nontraditional students—those aged 25 and older or those who do not enroll full time in higher education directly after high school—have presented a different problem for higher education. Over time, these students have begun to replace traditional students as the majority on college campuses. Between 1976 and 1986, nontraditional students grew from 40 to 48 percent of the total, and they are expected to total 60 percent by 2000 *(Policy Perspectives* 1990). Colleges and universities have responded to this growing segment by increasing their marketing efforts to attract such individuals to their campuses. Some observers have noted that despite these marketing efforts, higher education remains an enterprise tailored to the needs of traditional students (*Policy Perspectives* 1990). Thus, as these students become the new majority, they will begin to pose budgetary implications for the state, such as funding for new instructional programs, additional funding for off-campus sites, and a different orientation toward student services. Like achievement for minority students, ample literature exists on the trend in nontraditional students and their implications. But given the significance of the issue, the literature is extremely sparse with regard to specific state initiatives designed to improve the matriculation of nontraditional students.

The State and Independent Higher Education

State policy makers have long realized that the independent sector of higher education represents an important component of the diversity of higher education and that it also provides a number of economic, cultural, and other quality-of-life benefits to the state. One important direct benefit to some states has been the avoidance of costs to educate residents who choose to attend independent colleges and universities (Brinkman 1988). Consequently, some states have chosen to invest a significant amount in the independent sector. The significance of independent higher education varies considerably from state to state, given its physical presence and historical traditions. As a percentage of total higher education institutions, private institutions range from 88 percent in the District of Columbia to zero in Wyoming (Lapovsky and Allard 1986). As a result, the importance of the independent sector in the state higher education budget process varies from state to state as well.

Three distinct state policies can be discerned with regard to independent higher education (Zumeta 1988a). The first posture is the *laissez-faire approach*, in which the independent sector is left to its own resources and the state allows the sector to regulate itself. In extreme cases, the state provides no funding at all to these institutions. The second posture is *state central planning*, in which the independent sector is an integral part of state planning for higher education. At the opposite end from the laissez-faire posture, this approach extensively involves independent higher education in programmatic initiatives and is a recipient of substantial state dollars. In states practicing this posture, accountability is likely to be an important issue as well. The third posture is the *market-competitive approach,* whose basic policy objective is the promotion of fair competition between sectors. A state taking this posture would be most concerned with correcting "market imperfections" through subsidies for student aid, tax incentives, and other such mechanisms (Zumeta 1988a).

For states that have chosen to take a proactive policy stance toward independent higher education, the primary budgetary mechanisms have been student aid and direct institutional grants. All states except Wyoming (which has no independent institutions) now have at least one student aid program for students from the independent sector. In addition, 17 states have separate tuition equalization grant programs for students attending private institutions (Zumeta 1988b). In general, the proportion of a state's enrollment in private institutions and the level of funding for state student aid are strongly correlated (Zumeta and Green 1987). Given the decrease over time in federal financial aid and the significant increase in expenditures for institutional aid within the independent sector, state student financial aid programs (when linked with public university tuition policy) have probably become the most important policy lever available to state policy makers with regard to the private sector. Twenty-one states also have direct institutional grant programs to private colleges and universities that take the form of general aid (six states), support for health-related programs (21 states), support for other educational programs (12 states), support for research and technology (10 states), support for programs for underserved students (six states), support for cooperative ventures (four states), and capital grant programs (three states). The cumulative policy effect of direct institutional aid to the independent sector is less clear than that of state student aid, although the independent sector reportedly highly values direct state aid (Zumeta 1988b).

Summary
The state higher education budget has become an important means for implementing state-level higher education initiatives. Accountability has become a significant priority for state policy makers. As the concept of accountability has evolved from a fiduciary orientation to one directed toward outcomes,

accountability mechanisms have begun to evolve from reporting mechanisms to instruments of change or, in other words, from process to product. As a result, future accountability mechanisms will likely be more integrated into the state budget process for the purposes of feedback than at any time in the past.

Cost, productivity, and quality are inextricably linked. The significant growth in higher education costs is a function of the lack of internal constraints on resources, the labor-intensiveness of higher education, the natural propensity for colleges and universities to grow rather than reallocate, and the resulting organizational inefficiency. Related is the concern about the lack of productivity in higher education. At the same time that costs are increasing, the outcomes of higher education are becoming harder to measure, largely because goals are diffuse and unclear. Consequently, the maintenance of quality in higher education has become an extremely political issue for states. In an effort to maintain quality, several states have devised incentive funding programs to promote quality in specific areas, including undergraduate education and basic research. Related issues remaining for state policy makers include the setting of specific goals for higher education and the introduction of innovation within the budget process to meet those goals.

As the inequity between tuition and income increased during the 1980s, affordability began to take on importance as well. In an effort to maintain affordability, some states have attempted to link tuition policies to external factors rather than to the standard practice of using tuition revenues to offset declining state appropriations. Another way of addressing affordability through the budget process has been the funding of state student aid programs. States with high tuition usually have high student aid programs, although surprisingly few states closely link student aid, tuition, and institutional support. Several states have devised tuition prepayment and savings plans, and although they have high political appeal, they have several disadvantages, not the least of which is the lack of any evaluation of effectiveness. It is evident that states need to begin to coordinate their financing policies more efficiently if they are to effectively address the issue of affordability.

Higher education has become very involved in states' economic development, partially as a way to increase its funding from the state. State-funded economic development activities include research and development programs, involvement in educating and training the work force, and fostering partnerships with business for the purpose of technology transfer. The effectiveness of these activities remains unclear, and numerous potential problems exist, including the highly political nature of economic development and the fundamental differences between higher education and business.

Minority and nontraditional students present special problems for state policy makers. Minorities have increased as a percentage of the total population but have declined as a percentage of enrollments in higher education. Most states have initiated programs through the budget process to provide aid for minorities and to encourage the development of innovative cooperative programs within the education community. It is well accepted that nontraditional students are fast becoming the new majority in higher education, but higher education has done little to change its structure to meet the needs of nontraditional students.

Many states have long realized that the presence of independent higher education provides many tangible and intangible benefits. As a result, many states support the independent sector through student aid and institutional aid programs. Because federal student aid has decreased over time and institutional aid programs at private schools have increased, state aid programs probably represent the most significant policy lever available with regard to the independent sector.

ANALYSIS AND IMPLICATIONS

As previous sections have illustrated, state budgeting for higher education is a complex, multifaceted process involving a number of players and factors. Within the framework presented, the environmental context frames the state higher education budget process, resulting in a "product" (the budget), which in turn provides a number of outcomes. Synthesizing the literature on this and related topics provides a sense of the gaps in the knowledge related to state budgeting for higher education. This section analyzes the extent of what is known regarding this topic and the implications for research and for practitioners.

Analysis and Implications for Research

This subsection blends an analysis of what has been presented in this monograph with regard to state budgeting for higher education with the implications for research. It proceeds with the areas of framework used in this monograph as well as the separate areas of context, process, and product.

The framework for state-level budgeting for higher education

The framework for the budgetary process provides a start-to-finish, external environment–to–completed outcomes means of understanding what occurs in budgeting. The major weakness in the framework is empirical research to affirm (or disaffirm) portions of it. For example, research exists about the relationship between specific environmental factors and total state spending for higher education, but little research is available about the interactions among some of the environmental variables themselves and their combined effects on higher education budgets. The economic context of budgeting has already been established as a significant factor with regard to budget outcomes, but that economic context will be affected by the demographic and political factors that develop in the 1990s. One such factor is the aging of the population in general. Will older Americans desire higher education to the degree that once was supportable? As baby boomers age, will new political factors force shifts in the level and type of funding for higher education? The birth and coming of age of the baby boom generation forced massive expansion of higher education and its funding support during the 1960s and 1970s. Will it nosedive in the 1990s and into the next century as that same generation ages and requires a different set of services?

The environmental context of state budgeting for higher education

Within the scheme of state budgeting for higher education, contextual factors, such as a state's historical traditions, political culture, demography, and economy, all affect the process and outcomes. The historical traditions and political culture within a state provide the ground rules in the budget process, while demographics and the economy serve as immediate indicators of supply and demand for state services. A state's traditions and political culture indicate how much higher education is and has been viewed as a priority and the relative importance of the players within the budget process—the governor, legislature, state coordinating board, and individual campuses. On the other hand, demographics indicate the demand for state services, and the economy provides a measure of resources available to meet those needs.

Throughout the 1980s and as we move into the 1990s, it appears that the most critical contextual factor will be a state's economy, while other factors will moderate the effect of the economy on the process and outcomes. In the last decade, the prosperity of higher education both rose and fell with state economies. Because both the timing and the size of these changes vary from state to state, historical traditions, political culture, and demographics moderate the effects of the economy to some extent. To what degree these contextual factors interact separately and with the budget process is essentially unknown.

The culture and traditions of states are probably the most promising areas for looking at the effects of historical or political variables. As noted earlier, the research on the relationship between political variables and spending for higher education shows frustratingly inconclusive results. It is obvious to any observer of the political scene that variables like participation by voters, public opinion, or partisan control of the legislature influence a state's spending priorities. The traditional ways of measuring these factors' effects is clearly unsatisfactory. Conducting qualitative research on the culture and traditions, particularly some of the political traditions, may be a means of clarifying some of these relationships.

The state higher education budget process

Closely related to the culture and traditions of states is the *process* of budgeting, clearly an area that needs more research.

Budgeting and budgets cannot be captured entirely through numerical descriptions or quantitative studies. A budget is not cut and dried. It represents a wide spectrum of personalities, organizations, priorities, and needs. The study of budgeting does not support the English scientist Lord Kelvin's thesis (paraphrased) that "if it can be measured it can be understood." Merely measuring the budget in quantitative terms is not sufficient to tell the whole story of budgeting.

Merely measuring the budget in quantitative terms is not sufficient to tell the whole story.

Because of this factor and numerous environmental changes, budgeting cannot be described as simple incrementalism. Budgeting processes and outcomes are more complex than an annual linear progression. By understanding when deviations from incrementalism occur, one can begin to examine the events that occurred near that time that might be used to help explain the deviations. For example, state budgets for higher education do not follow a single straight line (Lyddon 1989); rather, the regression line is a series of smaller lines that shift at particular points. Identifying events such as the election of a new governor, a change in partisan control in the legislature, or other events might help explain what occurred before the shift and thus lend clues as to why the shift occurred.

The shift from incrementalism, in which budgets are largely based on what was decided in the past, to a market model of budgeting, in which budgets are adjusted to accommodate changing conditions, may vary state to state. This variation may happen as much because of the variation of economic conditions as because of political culture and traditions. It is not well understood what traditions govern why higher education in particular gets its "share" in good times or in bad. Do traditions or patterns of organizational types exist with respect to state budgeting for higher education? Some important work in this area (Fisher 1988a, 1988b) needs to be extended to other states and to specific state budgeting situations.

Considerable research on budgeting processes has occurred at the federal level. Such research models could be applied to states—individually or several at a time. For example, one could apply the examination of agenda setting in health care policy and transportation at the federal level (Kingdon 1984) to states and examine who sets agendas for different areas of the budget. Using research about the governor's role in budgeting (typically setting the parameters, or the agenda, for the state budget for higher education) (Adler and Lane 1988), one can study to what extent, and under what circumstances, higher education leaders are able to set the agenda or influence the agenda for higher education budgeting and how this agenda is affected by the presence of special interest groups. In many states, the advent of faculty unions and state-level student associations has become an addition to the equation. Though these interests are typically narrow (for example, faculty salaries and tuition costs), these groups have become another force tugging at the budget from different directions. Other increasingly powerful interest groups include community college associations and private college federations. A less organized, though quite potent, force is public opinion. Public opinion polls help governors, legislators, and some interest groups gauge citizens' reactions to policy and budgetary initiatives and therefore further affect the parameters of budgeting.

Analysis of interest groups and agenda setting in state higher education budgeting is not merely of theoretical interest. The lifeblood of higher education, especially public higher education, is state funding. Knowing who sets agendas and how within the political process can greatly enhance higher education's chances of influencing those agendas. Higher education as a budgetary priority ebbs and flows, yet its financial needs follow different patterns. Thus, it is critically important to understand the setting of, and influencing of, public policy agendas at the state level.

Research on the process of budgeting could draw heavily on decision theory and on organizational theory. Much literature is available in public administration about aspects of budgeting, including the budgeting process. It could be drawn together to assist in conducting research on state budgeting for higher education specifically. As already pointed out, the research literature on state budgeting for other areas is not completely applicable to state budgeting for higher education. Higher education has special relationships with states that may create completely different budgeting processes from other state government entities. In Illinois, for example, the governor allocates funds for each of the state agencies in his budget but provides a lump sum to the Board of Higher Education to distribute funds among the various sectors of higher education. In Michigan (as in other states), the final budget includes a lump sum for each institution of higher education, while the budgets for state agencies include very specific line items and numbers of FTE positions.

A useful area of research would be an examination of the role of legislative staffs in the budget process. Over time legislative staffers have become increasingly professional in their training and background. Legislative staffs have an effect in two major ways: (1) by acting as liaison between special interests and legislators and (2) though the staff members' abilities to specialize in a narrower issue or area than legislators can. Legislators might, for example, assign a staff person to get a sense of various special interests' views and to suggest a compromise or alternatives. Staff members' abilities to specialize (compared to legislators who must confront many issues) can influence budgeting through greater use of data, more ability to draw ideas, and resources from other states or other sources. The effect may offset elected officials' more political models of decision making by using rational sources of information and suggesting related styles of decision making. How does it affect state budgeting for higher education? When and how do staff members use their influence with policy makers? As legislatures in general are asserting their authority, it would be wise to examine their roles and those of the staff.

Another line of research is the effect of tight economic times on the budget *process*. The outcomes have changed during economic distress: Less money is available generally, and higher education has been viewed as more discretionary than other items in the state budget. Literature already exists about the effect of limited resources on institutions of higher education. In general, their budgeting becomes more centralized. Does the same phenomenon occur at the state level? What specifically goes into the decisions made by state officials to reduce spending for higher education (or to maintain its level) in tight economic times? Does the previous experience that higher education is more discretionary continue to hold true? Higher education is being incorporated into many states' efforts at economic revitalization. Will doing so help insulate the institutions from budget cuts in tight economic times?

The state higher education budget as policy document

To many state policy makers, the state budget for higher education is a way to link the state's policy priorities for higher

education with the resources needed to meet those goals and objectives. In the past, some policy makers have also used funding for higher education to further their own political goals, which might include both broad, statewide initiatives like involvement in economic development and assisting parents in saving for college and narrower goals, such as supporting the campus within one's home district (or withholding support from the campus in another's district). Some of the policy areas addressed through the budget for higher education include accountability, costs, productivity, and quality, affordability, economic development, minority and nontraditional students, and independent higher education.

Over time, the issue of accountability has evolved from a fiduciary orientation to one focused more on outcomes. Policy makers are increasingly interested in the goals achieved through the expenditure of state funds for higher education. Unfortunately, most of the current accountability mechanisms in place tend to stress the collection of substantial amounts of data for ambiguous or unknown objectives, resulting in continued dissatisfaction about the accountability of higher education to the state. It is evident that new accountability mechanisms will have to be designed in tandem with budgeting processes that consciously link funding with state objectives for higher education and also the performance of higher education with respect to achieving these goals. No doubt many institutional officials will resist such efforts. Institutions that speak the same language as state officials, however, often fare better in achieving new resources from the state.

Policy makers are also beginning to consider higher education's costs, productivity, and quality within the context of the budget. During the 1980s, costs of higher education grew at a rate far exceeding the rest of the economy as a result of the general lack of constraints on resources, its labor-intensity, and the propensity of colleges and universities to grow rather than to reallocate. Concurrent with the growth in costs has been growing concern about productivity. Higher education outcomes have generally remained ambiguous, while, at the same time, expenditures for higher education have increased, largely because of new revenues brought in through increased tuition rates. The natural results have been concerns about efficiency and quality.

Some states have implemented fiscal incentive programs as a means to "improve" or "maintain" quality, but the effectiveness of these programs is generally unclear. What is clear is the need for each state to devise a system that sets specific goals for quality and productivity and links state funding with these goals. In truth, not much in this system is different from what was originally described as the basic objective of budgeting: linking resources with policy objectives.

It is not yet clear whether the new quality initiatives represent either new funds to institutions or are a way to prevent funds from being eroded from state spending for higher education. It is also unclear what effect quality initiatives have on different institutions. Further, what organizational mechanisms help (or hinder) states' efforts to differentiate among institutions? That is, are quality initiatives spread evenly among all institutions or all programs, or are they rewards for actual performance and thereby differentiated according to level or performance outcomes? Which state entity decides on the distribution, and what effect does the decision maker have on the outcome?

State policy makers have also addressed the affordability of higher education through the budget. The traditional means of addressing affordability through the budget have been through tuition policies and student financial aid programs. Interestingly, very few states have attempted to integrate their institutional aid, tuition, and student aid policies into a cohesive program of support. In recent years, many states have also tried to address the issue of affordability through tuition prepayment and savings programs. These programs have high political appeal, though they have several practical disadvantages, not the least of which is the unpredictability of future levels of tuition. The effectiveness of these types of programs is currently unknown, and the area is ripe for further study.

The involvement of higher education in state economic development was a phenomenon of the 1980s. Ways that states have involved higher education in these efforts include research programs, training and education programs for the work force, and the development of partnerships between higher education and business for the purpose of technology transfer. Given the newness of these types of initiatives, their effectiveness remains ambiguous and potential political problems exist for higher education. Some evidence exists, however, that higher education reaps financial benefits in states where it plays a significant role in economic development. Questions remain about these programs' practical value. Is the payoff greater than the cost to the higher education institution or the state? Does spending for these programs continue ad infinitum, either as categorical programs or by being folded into the base budget itself, or are these programs subject to ongoing evaluation? What effect, if any, do these programs have on an institution's mission and program mix?

Through the higher education budget, state policy makers have also tried to address the issues of minority students' achievement and enrollment of nontraditional students. The effectiveness of current state programs—especially in the area of minority students' achievement—has been generally inconclusive, which suggests that either better mechanisms of evaluation need to be developed or that substantive programmatic problems exist. Further, information is lacking regarding the progress of nontraditional students in higher education, which is curious given the fact that these students are the new majority at many institutions. The information that does exist suggests that institutions are doing little more than tailoring the marketing of their schools to meet the perceived desires of these students while ignoring the need to change fundamentally the higher education delivery system. The potential for research here is limitless. Further, state sources pay little attention to nontraditional students. What budget mechanisms have been or can be used to deal with their needs?

In essence, the state higher education budget as policy document has shifted its orientation over time from that of providing resources to institutions through base budgets to a newer focus on designing categorical programs to meet the state's policy goals for higher education. Part of the reason may be that the increased state presence in higher education policy making has created this new emphasis on distinct programs. Part of it may be purely political in that as legislators become more professional and attuned to the educational needs of their constituencies, they may realize the value of being able to point out their particular contribution to a popular program. Again, the relative merit of using categorical programs versus base budgets to achieve the state's policy goals has not been evaluated and thus remains inconclusive. Similarly, little is available to suggest the source of the pressure to shift the focus from increasing the base to spreading funds into categorical programs. Initially, it appears that institutions prefer funds to flow into the base budget with few strings attached. As growth in the base budgets slowed and emphasis increased for categorical programs, however, some institutions have become quite adept at garnering resources through this mechanism. What impact does doing so have on other institutions that are not so adept?

On a broader scale, questions remain about the trend in funding higher education institutions through categorical programs as opposed to base budgets. Do certain patterns of categorical funding occur with regularity or predictability from which states or institutions can benefit? The relationship between categorical programs and the base also has room for examination. To what extent are categorical programs funded with the stated expectation of matching money for from the institution's base budget?

It is important to recognize that some sort of base, which provides continuity, must be maintained. Higher education is an enterprise that changes slowly, and to maintain important commitments to people and programs, institutions need a reasonable guarantee that their base budgets will be adequate to meet ongoing demands. Items not in the base budget are typically addressed as "categorical incentive programs" designed to meet specific state goals. Even these categorical programs, however, behave like base budgets over time. Increasingly, when individuals begin to consider categorical incentive programs as *entitlements,* the incentive is lost and little difference then exists between a categorical program and a base budget.

Projects like improving research capacity or improving retention of underrepresented minority students take time. Including incentives as categorical programs stimulates change within higher education. Including them as categorical programs with a too-short time span to accomplish real change is a recipe for failure. Thus, state policy makers are challenged to extend their time perspectives. Just as important is the challenge to higher education to speed up the pace a bit. Saying that higher education changes slowly does not mean to suggest that all change is good or that speed is necessarily a virtue. Numerous societal problems, however, require faster action on the part of higher education institutions. In such instances, categorical funding is probably the best funding mechanism as long as such programs remain incentives and are not allowed to become entitlements.

In general, then, it is evident that the potential for policy research on state budgeting for higher education is enormous.

. . . budgeting is a ritual, albeit a ritual with changing externalities, participants and desired outcomes.

Little literature available in public administration and political science refers specifically either to states or to state budgeting for higher education. Although this monograph shies away from anecdotal information, such information is a mother lode from which to start research. It is generally localized to a state, a time span, or a particular budget area and must then be tested and broadened beyond pure localism.

Implications for Practitioners

One of the real benefits of synthesizing the literature on state budgeting for higher education is the opportunity to present a list of implications and recommendations for practitioners in the field. Having said that, the authors must now admit that because they do not view budgeting as a mechanized activity to be learned in "cookbook" fashion, no grand list of secrets is available to present to practitioners to enhance their funding base or improve their success (or conversely, minimize their losses) in the process. Nor is it desirable. If this monograph has illustrated one point, it is that state budgeting for higher education is a complex process.

What is presented in this monograph is a synthesis that portrays the major forces and factors internal and external to the budgetary process. The single most important implication or recommendation that can be offered to practitioners is that all participants, from the state-level agency to the department within an institution, should be aware of all the parts of the big picture of state budgeting for higher education. It above all is the first and most important step in understanding state budgeting for higher education and perhaps in improving one's effectiveness in achieving objectives in the process.

State Budgeting for Higher Education as Enigma, Paradox, and Ritual

The title of this monograph suggests that state budgeting for higher education is an enigma, a paradox, and a ritual. For many, budgeting in general is an enigma. Certainly for the uninitiated, it is. Few guideposts are available in state budgeting for higher education. Information is available about outcomes of budgeting, some literature about the process. Mostly, however, what is available are millions of anecdotal tales from experienced professionals. Some are willing to share the stories, enabling the researcher to begin piecing together a more complete understanding of budgeting. That, combined with further reading and work within the field can help, for budgeting has many interwoven parts.

Budgeting is paradoxical. Traditional budgeteers have approached the subject as a set of columns and rows of numbers that must properly add up within limited state revenues. More recently, however, persons with other disciplinary backgrounds have begun noting that budgeting is much more than that. It is both simple and complex. The simple parts of budgeting can be represented as a broad framework with inputs, a process of manipulating those inputs, and outputs. The complexities are the details. A more important paradox is that although both practitioners and scholars insist that the primary purpose of state budgeting for higher education is to link state intentions with desired policy outcomes, little evidence exists to suggest that this purpose is being met.

This monograph tries both to simplify some aspects of the budgeting process and product and to represent fairly the many complexities of it. At the same time, it tries to note that the outcomes are not always as they seem. For example, state legislators quickly look to the bottom line percentage increase for each institution. They compare the increase of "their" institution with those of others. The percentage increase from year to year is a simple means of assessing how well an institution is doing. The legislators all know, however, that the simple percentage increase from year to year has greater implications. The percentage increase can appeal to voters back home, it can include mostly general operating funds or funds with considerable strings attached, or it can represent a large percentage built on a small base or a smaller percentage on a large base.

Finally, budgeting is a ritual, albeit a ritual with changing externalities, participants, and desired outcomes. Like the theme music in a symphony, certain budgeting actions are repeated in the same or a slightly different form throughout the process. The cycles of the budget process are repeated again and again for many years. In many cases, the outcomes are the same from year to year as well. To some extent, it is a result of comfortable rituals. Budgeting is a process, and despite changes in externalities, participants, and desired policy outcomes, it always will be a process. Thus, state budgeting for higher education will remain inherently ritualistic.

As we move through the 1990s, higher education policy makers and practitioners at both the state and institutional level will be facing significant pressures to improve upon the ways higher education addresses the needs of citizens within the state. Clearly, the state budget process should be the means by which improvements are made in both policy outcomes and the delivery of services to the citizenry. Given that the process is demonstrably complex and that we need to know much more about it, it is evident that great potential exists for an improved level of consciousness about state budgeting for higher education through a strengthened link between research and practice.

REFERENCES

The Educational Resources Information Center (ERIC) Clearinghouse on Higher Education abstracts and indexes the current literature on higher education for inclusion in ERIC's data base and announcement in ERIC's monthly bibliographic journal, *Resources in Education* (RIE). Most of these publications are available through the ERIC Document Reproduction Service (EDRS). For publications cited in this bibliography that are available from EDRS, ordering number and price code are included. Readers who wish to order a publication should write to the ERIC Document Reproduction Service, 3900 Wheeler Avenue, Alexandria, Virginia 22304. (Phone orders with VISA or MasterCard are taken at 800/227-ERIC or 703/823-0500.) When ordering, please specify the document (ED) number. Documents are available as noted in microfiche (MF) and paper copy (PC). If you have the price code ready when you call EDRS, an exact price can be quoted. The last page of the latest issue of *Resources in Education* also has the current cost, listed by code.

Abney, Glenn, and Thomas P. Lauth. 1986. "The Politics of State and City Administration." In *Public Administration in the 1980s,* edited by Peter Colby. Albany, N.Y.: SUNY Press.

Adams, C.R. 1977. "Information Technology: Performance and Promise." In *Appraising Information Needs of Decision Makers,* edited by Carl R. Adams. New Directions for Institutional Research No. 15. San Francisco: Jossey-Bass.

Adams, L.R. 1988. "A Corporate View: The Information Revolution." *State Government News.* Lexington, Ky.: Council of State Governments.

Adler, M.W., and F.S Lane. 1988. "Governors and Public Policy Leadership." In *Governors and Higher Education,* edited by S. Gove and T. Beyle. Denver: Education Commission of the States.

Albritton, Robert B., and Ellen M. Dran. 1987. "Balanced Budgets and State Surpluses: The Politics of Budgeting in Illinois." *Public Administration Review* 47: 143–52.

Allen, R. 1980. "A Preliminary Report on the National Survey of State Resource Allocation." In *Financing and Budgeting Postsecondary Education in the 1980s,* edited by L.L. Leslie and H.L. Otto. Tucson: Univ. of Arizona, Center for the Study of Higher Education. ED 197 668. 95 pp. MF–01; PC–04.

Allen, R.H. 1984. "New Approaches to Incentive Financing." In *Responding to New Realities in Funding,* edited by L.L. Leslie. San Francisco: Jossey-Bass.

Allen, R.H., and J.R. Topping. 1979. *Cost Information and Formula Funding: New Approaches.* Boulder, Colo.: National Center for Higher Education Management Systems. ED 183 057. 77 pp. MF–01; PC–04.

Anderson, Richard E. 1988a. "College Savings and Prepayment Plans." *Capital Ideas* 2(3–4): 1–15.

———. 1988b. "The Economy and Higher Education." *Capital Ideas* 1(3): 1–11.

———. 1988c. "Tax-Exempt College Savings Bonds: Problems and Solutions." In *States and the Bond Markets,* edited by R. Snell and T. Hutchison. Denver: National Conference of Legislators.

Anderson, Richard E., and William Massy. 1989. "The Economic Outlook and What It Means for Colleges and Universities." *Capital Ideas* 4(3): 1–10.

Berdahl, Robert O., and Susan M. Studds. 1989. "The Tension of Excellence and Equity: The Florida Enhancement Programs." Paper presented at the National Center for Postsecondary Governance and Finance Conference on State Fiscal Incentives, November, Denver, Colorado.

Berne, Robert, and Richard Schramm. 1986. *The Financial Analysis of Governments.* Englewood Cliffs, N.J.: Prentice-Hall.

BeVier, M.J. 1979. *Politics Backstage: Inside the California Legislature.* Philadelphia: Temple Univ. Press.

Beyle, Thad L. 1983. "Governors." In *Politics in the American States: A Comparative Analysis,* edited by V. Gray, H. Jacob, and K. Vines. 4th ed. Boston: Scott, Foresman & Co.

———. 1985. "Higher Education and the 1985 State of the State Addresses." In *Governors and Higher Education: A Partnership for the Future.* Racine, Wisc.: Proceedings of the Wingspread Conference. ED 284 455. 52 pp. MF–01; PC–03.

Biemiller, L. 19 June 1985. "How the University of Texas, Flexing Its Political Muscle, Foiled Budget Cutters." *Chronicle of Higher Education:* 12–15.

Bird, Barbara J., and David N. Allen. 1989. "Faculty Entrepreneurship in Research University Environments." *Journal of Higher Education* 60(5): 583–96.

Bowen, Howard R. 1980. *The Costs of Higher Education.* San Francisco: Jossey-Bass.

Bowman, Mary J. 1985. "Education, Population Trends, and Technological Change." *Economics of Education Review* 4(1): 29–44.

Brandl, John E. 1988. "The Legislative Role in Policy Making for Higher Education." In *Governors and Higher Education,* edited by S. Gove and T. Beyle. Denver: Education Commission of the States.

Brazier, H.E. 1982. "An Anatomy of a Fiscal Crisis: The Michigan Case." *Public Budgeting and Finance* 2(4): 130–42.

Breneman, D.W., and S.C. Nelson. 1981. *Financing Community Colleges: An Economic Perspective.* Washington, D.C.: Brookings Institution.

Brinkman, Paul. 1984. "Formula Budgeting: The Fourth Decade." In *Responding to New Realities in Funding,* edited by L.L. Leslie. San Francisco: Jossey-Bass.

———. 1988. "The Costs of Providing Higher Education: A Conceptual Overview." Denver: State Higher Education Executive Officers.

Brubacher, John S., and Willis Rudy. 1976. *Higher Education in Transition.* 3d rev. ed. New York: Harper & Row.

Business Week. 25 September 1989. "The New America" 3125: 90–179.

Cage, Mary C. 31 May 1989a. "After Two Years of Opposition, Key Legislator in Illinois Decides to Back Tax Rise for Colleges." *Chronicle of Higher Education* 35: 14.

————. 31 May 1989b. "Louisiana's Public Colleges Fear the State's Budget Struggle Will Lead to More Campus Cuts." *Chronicle of Higher Education* 35: 15.

Caiden, Naomi. 1988. "Shaping Things to Come: Super-Budgeters as Heroes (and Heroines) in the Late Twentieth Century." In *New Directions in Budget Theory,* edited by I.S. Rubin. Albany, N.Y.: SUNY Press.

Caiden, Naomi, and J. Chapman. 1982. "Constraint and Uncertainty: Budgeting in California." *Public Budgeting and Finance* 2(4): 111–29.

California Postsecondary Education Commission. 1990. "Higher Education at the Crossroads: Planning for the 21st Century." Sacramento: Author.

Carlisle, E.F. 1988. "A Random Walk through Assessment: The Perspective of an Academic Affairs Officer." Presentation for the Univ. of Wisconsin System Conference on Assessment, January, Madison, Wisconsin.

Carlisle, E.R. 1988. "Educating for the Future." *Planning and Changing* 19(3): 131–40.

Carnevale, John T. Summer 1988. "Recent Trends in the Finances of the State and Local Sector." *State and Local Finances:* 33–48.

Caruthers, J. Kent, and Melvin Orwig. 1979. *Budgeting in Higher Education.* AAHE-ERIC Higher Education Report No. 3. Washington, D.C.: American Association for Higher Education. ED 169 875. 110 pp. MF–01; PC–05.

Caruthers, J. Kent, and Joseph Marks. 1988. "State Funding of Higher Education for Quality Improvement in the SREB States." Atlanta: Southern Regional Education Board. ED 305 011. 64 pp. MF–01; PC–03.

Chronicle of Higher Education. 5 September 1990. "California." In *Almanac: Facts about Higher Education in the Nation, State, and D.C.:* 32–33.

Committee on Scope, Structure, and Productivity of Illinois Higher Education. 1990. "An Action Agenda for Illinois Higher Education: Improving Quality, Cost Effectiveness, and Accountability in the 1990s." Springfield: Illinois Board of Higher Education.

Conrad, Clifton F., and Richard F. Wilson. 1985. *Academic Program Reviews: Institutional Approaches, Expectations, and Controversies.* ASHE-ERIC Higher Education Report No. 5. Washington, D.C.: As-

sociation for the Study of Higher Education. ED 264 806. 111 pp.
MF–01; PC–05.

Coughlin, Cletus C., and O. Homer Erekson. 1986. "Determinants
of State Aid and Voluntary Support of Higher Education." *Economics of Education Review* 5(2): 179–90.

Crosson, Patricia H. 1983. "The Pennsylvania Postsecondary Education System: Coping with Enrollment and Resource Declines."
Journal of Higher Education 54(5): 533–51.

Curry, Denis J. 1988. "Financing the Student Costs of Higher Education: Considerations for Effective Access." Working Paper.
Denver: Education Commission of the States.

Curry, Denis J., and Norman Fischer. 1986. "Public Higher Education
and the State: Models for Financing, Budgeting, and Accountability." Paper presented at an annual meeting of the Association
for the Study of Higher Education, February, San Antonio, Texas.
ED 268 886. 36 pp. MF–01; PC–02.

Curry, Denis J., Norman Fischer, and Tom Jons. 1982. *State Policy
Options for Financing Higher Education and Related Accountability Objectives: Summary and Conclusions.* Olympia: Washington Council for Postsecondary Education.

Davis, N.M. 1984. "Legislative Staff Careers." *State Legislatures* 10(10):
11–18.

Davis, O.A., M.A. Dempster, and Aaron Wildavsky. 1966. "A Theory
of the Budgetary Process." *American Political Science Review*
60(3): 529–47.

Davis, William E. 9 March 1988a. "The Growing Politicization of State
Higher Education Makes Jobs of Top College Officials Shakier than
Ever." *Chronicle of Higher Education* 34: 52.

———. 1988b. "Presidential Perspectives." *Green Sheet.* Washington,
D.C.: National Association of State Universities and Land-Grant
Colleges.

Dawson, R.E., and J.A. Robinson. 1963. "Interparty Competition, Economic Variables, and Welfare Policies in the American States." *Journal of Politics* 25(2): 265–89.

Dionne, E.J., Jr. 22 March 1979. "Two Albany Aides Play Key Role in
State Budget Battle." *New York Times.*

Duncombe, Sydney, and Richard Kinney. 1986. "The Politics of State
Appropriation Increases: The Perspective of Budget Officers
in Five Western States." *Journal of State Government* 59(3):
113–23.

Dye, Thomas R. 1966. *Politics, Economics, and the Public: Policy Outcomes in the American States.* Chicago: Rand McNally.

———. 1969. "Executive Power and Public Policy in the States." *Western Political Quarterly* 22: 926–39.

———. 1976. *Policy Analysis: What Governments Do, Why They Do
It, and What Difference It Makes.* Tuscaloosa: Univ. of Alabama
Press.

Dye, T.R., and J.S. Robey. 1980. "Politics versus Economics: Development of the Literature on Policy Determination." In *The Determinants of Public Policy,* edited by T.R. Dye and V. Gray. New York: Lexington Books.

Easton, D. 1957. "An Approach to the Analysis of Political Systems." *World Politics* 9: 383–400.

Economist. 24 July 1989a. "Life after Oil" 311(7607): 26+.

―――. 25 November 1989b. "Town versus Gown" 313(7630): 28.

El-Khawas, Elaine. 1988. "Campus Trends, 1988." Higher Education Panel Report No. 77. Washington, D.C.: Amercian Council on Education. ED 301 121. 70 pp. MF–01; PC–03.

Eulau, H. 1971. "Political Norms Affecting Decisions Concerning Higher Education." In *Higher Education for Everybody? Issues and Implications,* edited by W.T. Furniss.

Eulau, H., and H. Quinley. 1970. *State Officials and Higher Education.* Report for the Carnegie Commission on Higher Education. New York: McGraw-Hill.

Fabricant, S. 1952. *The Trend of Government Activity in the United States since 1900.* New York: National Bureau of Economic Research.

Feig, D.G. 1985. "Looking at Supreme Court Impact in Context: The Case of Reapportionment and State Spending." *American Politics Quarterly* 13: 167–87.

Fisher, G.W. 1964. "Interstate Variation in State and Local Government Expenditures." *National Tax Journal* 17: 57–64.

Fisher, Lois A. 1988a. "External Political Traditions: Their Development and Continuing Impact on the Nature of Two Public Systems of Higher Education." Paper presented at the 1988 Annual Meeting of the Association for the Study of Higher Education, November, St. Louis, Missouri.

―――. 1988b. "State Legislatures and the Autonomy of Colleges and Universities: A Comparative Study of Legislation in Four States, 1900–1979." *Journal of Higher Education* 59(2):133–62.

Floyd, Carol E. 1982. *State Planning, Budgeting, and Accountability: Approaches for Higher Education.* AAHE-ERIC Higher Education Report No. 6. Washington, D.C.: American Association for Higher Education. ED 224 452. 58 pp. MF–01; PC–03.

Folger, John, ed. 1984. *Financial Incentives for Academic Quality.* San Francisco: Jossey-Bass.

―――. 1989. "Designing State Incentive Programs that Work in Higher Education." Paper presented at the National Center for Postsecondary Governance and Finance Conference on State Fiscal Incentives, November, Denver, Colorado.

Folger, John, and Robert O. Berdahl. 1988. "Patterns in Evaluating State Higher Education Systems: Making a Virtue out of Necessity." Publication No. RR 87:3. College Park, Md.: National Center for Postsecondary Governance and Finance.

Fonte, Richard. 1989. "Financial Governance Patterns among Two-Year Colleges." Paper presented at a conference of the Association for the Study of Higher Education, November, Atlanta, Georgia. ED 313 990. 24 pp. MF–01; PC–01.

Frances, Carol. 1986. "Changing Enrollment Trends: Implications for the Future Financing of Higher Education." In *Values in Conflict: Funding Priorities for Higher Education,* edited by M. McKeown and K. Alexander. Cambridge, Mass.: Ballinger.

Garms, Walter I. 1986. "The Determinants of Public Revenues for Higher and Lower Education: A Thirty-Year Perspective." *Educational Evaluation and Policy Analysis* 8(3): 277–93.

Gilmour, J.E., Jr., and J.L. Suttle. 1984. "The Politics and Practicalities of Pricing in Academe." In *Issues in Pricing Undergraduate Education,* edited by L.H. Litten. New Directions for Institutional Research No. 42. San Francisco: Jossey-Bass.

Glenny, Lyman A. 1972. "The Anonymous Leaders of Higher Education." *Journal of Higher Education* 43: 9–22.

———. 1985. "State Coordination of Higher Education: The Modern Concept." Denver: State Higher Education Executive Officers. ED 270 070. 27 pp. MF–01; PC–02.

Gold, Steven D. 1987. "Developments in State Finances, 1983–1986." *Public Budgeting and Finance:* 5–23.

Gosling, J.J. 1987. "The State Budget Office and Policy Making." *Public Budgeting and Finance:* 51–65.

Green, K.C. 1986. "Government Responsibility for Quality and Equality in Higher Education." In *Policy Controversies in Higher Education,* edited by S.K. Gove and T. M. Stauffer. New York: Greenwood Press.

Green, M.B., and R. Riggs. 1988. *Performance Audit Report: Determining the Effect of Eliminative University Degrees and Programs.* Topeka, Kan.: Legislative Division of Post Audit.

Gross, F.M. 1973. "A Comparative Analysis of the Existing Budget Formula Used for Justifying Budget Requests or Allocating Funds for the Operating Expenses of State-supported Colleges and Universities." Knoxville: Univ. of Tennessee, Office of Institutional Research. ED 168 409. 158 pp. MF–01; PC–07.

Hairston, Elaine H. 1989. "State Fiscal Incentives in Higher Education: Ohio's Selective Excellence Program." Paper presented at the National Center for Postsecondary Governance and Finance Conference on State Fiscal Incentives, November, Denver, Colorado.

Hale, J.S., and T.M Rawson. 1976. "Developing Statewide Higher Education Funding Formulas for Use in a Limited-Growth Environment." *Journal of Education Finance* 2: 16–32.

Halstead, Kent. 1974. *Statewide Planning in Higher Education.* Washington, D.C.: U.S. Government Printing Office.

———. 1989a. *Higher Education Tuition.* Washington, D.C.: Research Associates of Washington.

————. 1989b. *State Profiles: Financing Public Higher Education, 1978–1989.* Washington, D.C.: Research Associates of Washington.

Hansen, Janet. 1989. "Student Financial Aid: Old Commitments, New Challenges." *College Board Review* 152: 29–31.

Harris, S.E., ed. 1964. *Economic Aspects of Higher Education.* Organisation for Economic Cooperation and Development.

Hartmark, Leif S. 1978. "The Effect of Rationalistic Budgeting and Legislative Staff upon University Policy-Making Independence: The Wisconsin Experience." Ph.D. dissertation, State Univ. of New York at Albany.

Hartmark, Leif S., and Edward R. Hines. 1986. "Politics and Policy in Higher Education: Reflections on the Status of the Field." In *Policy Controversies in Higher Education,* edited by S. Gove and T. Stauffer. New York: Greenwood Press.

Hauptman, Arthur. 1989. "Why Are College Charges Rising?" *College Board Review* 152: 11+.

Hearn, James C., and Melissa S. Anderson. 1989. "Integrating Postsecondary Education Financing Policies: The Minnesota Model." In *Studying the Impact of Student Aid on Institutions,* edited by R.H. Fenske. New Directions for Institutional Research No. 62. San Francisco: Jossey-Bass.

Herzik, Eric B. 1988. "The Expanding Gubernatorial Role in Education Policymaking." In *Governors and Higher Education,* edited by S. Gove and T. Beyle. Denver: Education Commission of the States.

Hines, Edward R. 1988a. *Higher Education and State Governments: Renewed Partnership, Cooperation, or Competition?* ASHE-ERIC Higher Education Report No. 5. Washington, D.C.: Association for the Study of Higher Education. ED 306 840. 117 pp. MF–01; PC–05.

————. November/December 1988b. "State Support of Higher Education: A Retrospective of FY 1989." *Grapevine* No. 350: 2207–12. Normal: Center for Higher Education at Illinois State Univ.

Hines, Edward R., and Leif Hartmark. 1980. *Politics of Higher Education.* AAHE-ERIC Higher Education Report No. 7. Washington, D.C.: American Association for Higher Education. ED 201 263. 85 pp. MF–01; PC–04.

Hines, Edward R., G. Alan Hickrod, and Gwen B. Pruyne. 1989. *State Support of Higher Education: From Expansion to Steady State to Decline, 1969–1989.* MacArthur/Spencer Series No. 9. Normal, Ill.: Center for Education Finance and Higher Education.

Jaschik, Scott. 13 July 1988. "Surge in Enrollment Poses Tricky Problem for U. of California." *Chronicle of Higher Education* 34: 17+.

Johnson, Lynn G. 1984. *The High-Technology Connection: Academic/Industrial Cooperation for Economic Growth.* ASHE-ERIC Higher Education Research Report No. 6. Washington, D.C.: Association for the Study of Higher Education. ED 255 130. 129 pp. MF–01;

PC–06.

Johnston, W.B., and Associates. 1987. *Workforce 2000: Work and Workers for the Twenty-first Century.* Indianapolis: Hudson Institute.

Jones, Dennis. 1984. *Higher Education Budgeting at the State Level: Concepts and Principles.* Boulder, Colo.: National Center for Higher Education Management Systems. ED 256 265. 120 pp. MF–01; PC–05.

———. 1989. "Financial Incentives and Budgeting Practices." Paper presented at the National Center for Postsecondary Governance and Finance Conference on State Fiscal Incentives, November, Denver, Colorado.

Jones, E.T. 1974. "Political Change and Spending Shifts in the American States." *American Politics Quarterly* 2: 159–78.

———. 1984. "Public Universities and the New State Politics." *Educational Record* 65(3): 10–12.

Jones, L.R. 1978. "Fiscal Strategies to Stimulate Instructional Innovation and Change." *Journal of Higher Education* 49(6): 588–607.

Kearney, Richard C. 1987. "How a Weak Governor Can Be Strong." *Journal of State Government* 60(4): 150–56.

Keenan, Boyd. 1987. "High Tech and Higher Education in DuPage: Testing the System of Systems." *Illinois Issues* 13(6): 1417.

Kim, Suk H., and Forrest W. Price. 1977. "Some Factors Affecting Public Spending on Public Higher Education." *Peabody Journal of Education* 54(4): 256–61.

Kingdon, John W. 1984. *Agendas, Alternatives, and Public Policies.* Boston: Little, Brown & Co.

Lamb, Jane A. 1986. "An Analysis of the Structure of 1985 State Budget Formulas for Public Higher Education with a Comparison of 1973, 1979, and 1985 Data." Ed.D. dissertation, Univ. of Tennessee.

Lapovsky, Lucie, and Sandra Allard. 1986. "State Support to Private Higher Education." In *Values in Conflict: Funding Priorities for Higher Education,* edited by M. McKeown and K. Alexander. Cambridge, Mass.: Ballinger.

Layzell, Daniel T. 1988a. "Pay Now, Pay Later: Is Prepayment Tuition the Answer?" *Educational Record* 69(3–4): 16–19.

———. 1988b. "The Relationship between Demographic, Economic, and Sociopolitical Factors and State Appropriations to Public Four-Year Colleges and Universities in Florida, Illinois, and Virginia: 1965–1985." Ph.D dissertation, Florida State Univ.

Lee, R.D., Jr., and R.W. Johnson. 1983. *Public Budgeting Systems.* 3d ed. Baltimore: University Park Press.

LeLoup, Lance T. 1988. "From Microbudgeting to Macrobudgeting: Evolution in Theory and Practice." In *New Directions in Budget Theory,* edited by I.S. Rubin. Albany, N.Y.: SUNY Press.

Leslie, David. 1987. "The Common Law of the Academic Profession:

An Assessment." *Review of Higher Education* 10(4): 295–318.

Leslie, Larry L. 1983. "Recent Financing Developments in the Fifty States." In *Survival in the 1980s: Quality, Mission, and Financing Options,* edited by Robert A. Wilson. Tucson: Center for the Study of Higher Education.

Leslie, Larry L., and Paul T. Brinkman. 1988. *The Economic Value of Higher Education.* New York: ACE/Macmillan.

Leslie, Larry L., and Garey Ramey. 1986. "State Appropriations and Enrollments: Does Enrollment Growth Still Pay?" *Journal of Higher Education* 57: 1–19.

Levin, Henry M. 1989. "Raising Productivity in Higher Education." *Policy Perspectives.* Philadelphia: Univ. of Pennsylvania, Higher Education Research Program.

Levy, Frank. 1989. "Paying for College: A New Look at Family Income Trends." *College Board Review* 152: 18+.

Lingenfelter, Paul E. 1974. "The Politics of Higher Education Appropriations in Three Midwestern States." Ph.D dissertation, Univ. of Michigan.

Lyddon, Jan W. 1989. "Incrementalism and Economic, Demographic, and Political Conditions Related to State Appropriations to Higher Education: A Study of the Fifty States from 1960 to 1985." PhD. dissertation, Univ. of Michigan.

Lyddon, Jan W., Richard Fonte, and James L. Miller. 1986. "Toward a Framework to Analyze State Funding of Higher Education." Paper presented at a meeting of the Association for the Study of Higher Education, February, San Diego, California.

McGuinness, Aims C., Jr. 1986. "The Search for More Effective State Policy Leadership in Higher Education." Working Paper PS-86-1. Denver: Education Commission of the States.

———. 1988. *State Postsecondary Education Structures Handbook, 1988.* Publication No. PS-87-2. Denver: Education Commission of the States. ED 305 849. 236 pp. MF–01; PC–10.

McGuinness, Aims C., and Christine Paulson. 1989. "1989 Survey of College Savings and Guaranteed Tuition Programs." Denver: Education Commission of the States. ED 317 144. 62 pp. MF–01; PC–03.

McKeown, Mary P. 1982. "The Use of Formulas for State Funding of Higher Education." *Journal of Education Finance* 7: 277–300.

———. 1986. "Funding Formulas." In *Values in Conflict: Funding Priorities for Higher Education,* edited by M. McKeown and K. Alexander. Cambridge, Mass.: Ballinger.

Maryland Higher Education Commission. 1988. "Guideline Use in Other States." Annapolis, Md.: Author.

Maryland State Board of Higher Education. 1986. "State Initiatives to Promote Technological Innovation and Economic Growth." Annapolis, Md.: Author.

Massachusetts Board of Regents of Higher Education. 1988. "A Margin for Excellence: A Tuition Policy for Public Higher Education in Massachusetts. A Statement of Principles and Policies." Boston, Mass.: Author. ED 299 847. 36 pp. MF–01; PC–02.

Massy, William F. 1989. "A Strategy for Productivity Improvement in College and University Academic Departments." Paper presented at the Forum for Postsecondary Governance, October, Santa Fe, New Mexico.

Maxwell, J.A., and J.R. Aronson. 1977. *Financing State and Local Governments.* 3d ed. Washington, D.C.: Brookings Institution.

Meisinger, R.J., Jr. 1976. *State Budgeting for Higher Education: The Uses of Formulas.* Berkeley: Univ. of California, Center for Research and Development in Higher Education. ED 132 963. 283 pp. MF–01; PC–12.

Michigan Department of State. 1971. *Michigan Manual, 1971–72.* Lansing: Dept. of Administration.

———. 1989. *Michigan Manual, 1989–90.* Lansing: Dept. of Administration.

Mikesell, John L. 1984. "The Cyclical Sensitivity of State and Local Taxes." *Public Budgeting and Finance* 4(1): 32–39.

Millard, Richard M. 1981. "Power of State Coordinating Agencies." In *Improving Academic Management: A Handbook of Planning and Institutional Research,* edited by Paul Jedamus and Marvin W. Peterson. San Francisco: Jossey-Bass.

Miller, James L., Jr. 1964. *State Budgeting for Higher Education: The Use of Formulas and Cost Analysis.* Ann Arbor: Univ. of Michigan, Institute of Public Administration.

Mitchell, J., R. Feiock, and D.S. Owen. 1985. "A Comparative Analysis of Government Growth in the Fifty American States: A Test of Five Explanations." Paper presented at an annual meeting of the Midwest Political Science Association, April, Chicago, Illinois.

Mingle, James R. 1988. "Survey on Tuition Policy, Costs, and Student Aid." Denver: State Higher Education Executive Officers. ED 299 878. 43 pp. MF–01; PC–02.

———. 1989. "The Political Meaning of Quality." *AAHE Bulletin* 41(9): 8–11. ED 308 748. 5 pp. MF–01; PC–01.

Mingle, James R., and Charles S. Lenth. 1989. "A New Approach to Accountability and Productivity in Higher Education." Denver: State Higher Education Executive Officers.

Morgan, Anthony W. 1984. "The New Strategies: Roots, Context, and Overview." In *Responding to New Realities in Funding,* edited by L.L. Leslie. San Francisco: Jossey-Bass.

Morss, E.R., J.E. Fredland, and S.H. Hymans. 1967. "Fluctuations in State Expenditures: An Econometric Analysis." *Southern Economic Journal.*

Mosher, F.C. and O.F. Poland. 1969. *The Costs of American Governments: Facts, Trends, Myths.* New York: Dodd, Mead & Co.

Moss, C.E., and G.H. Gaither. 1976. "Formula Budgeting: Requiem or Renaissance?" *Journal of Higher Education* 47: 543–63.

Mullen, J. Michael. 1988. "College Costs and the State Role in Higher Education Funding." *Educational Record* 69(3–4): 8–15.

Munitz, B., and R. Lawless. 1986. "Resource Allocation Policies for the Eighties." In *Policy Controversies in Higher Education*, edited by S.K. Gove and T. M. Stauffer. New York: Greenwood Press.

National Center for Higher Education Management Systems. 1988. "The Independent Sector's Public Purposes: Implications for State Policy Analysis." Publication No. PS-88-7. Denver: Education Commission of the States.

National Conference of State Legislatures. 1982. *Higher Education Finance Issues for the 1980s and 1990s: A Legislators' Handbook.* Denver: Author.

———. 1988. *State Legislative Report.* Denver: Author.

Nazario, Sonia L. 9 February 1990. "Bearing the Brunt." *Wall Street Journal*.

Noe, Roger C. 1986. "Formula Funding in Higher Education: A Review." *Journal of Education Finance* 11: 363–76.

Ohio Board of Regents. 1989. "Toward the Year 2000: Master Plan for Higher Education." Columbus: Author.

Oppenheimer, B.I. 1985. "Legislative Influence on Policy and Budgets." In *Handbook of Legislative Research*, edited by Gerhard Leowenberg, Samuel C. Patterson, and Malcolm E. Jewell Cambridge, Mass.: Harvard Univ. Press.

Paterson, A. May 1985. "Automating the State Legislatures." *State Legislatures*. 9–16.

Peacock, A.T., and J. Wiseman. 1961. *The Growth of Public Expenditures in the United Kingdom*. Princeton, N.J.: Princeton Univ. Press.

Peterson, Robert G. 1973. "Environmental and Political Determinants of Higher Education Appropriations Policies in the American States." Ph.D dissertation, Univ. of Michigan.

Pickens, William H. 1982. "Government Finance of Higher Education in the United States of America in the 1980s: Some Predictions and Perspectives." Paper presented at an international meeting of the Conference of Registrars and Secretaries and at the Conference of University Administrators of the United Kingdom, September, Hong Kong.

Pipho, Chris. 1989. "The Gap Widens: State Revenues Fall Short of Education Needs." *State Education Leader* 8(2): 1+.

Policy Perspectives. 1990. "Breaking the Mold" 2(2). Philadelphia: Univ. of Pennsylvania.

Reeher, Kenneth R., and Jerry S. Davis. 1988. "NASSGP Annual Survey Report, 1987–88 Academic Year." ED 296 640. 231 pp. MF-01; PC-10.

Rosensweig, Robert M. 28 February 1990. "Challenges to Test the Mettle of Academe's Best Leaders." *Chronicle of Higher Education*

36(25): 44.

Ruyle, J., and Lyman A. Glenny. 1979. *State Budgeting for Higher Education: Trends in State Revenue Appropriations from 1968 to 1977.* Berkeley, Cal.: Center for the Study of Higher Education. ED 192 637. 236 pp. MF–01; PC–10.

Sacks, S., and R. Harris. 1964. "The Determinants of State and Local Government Expenditures and Intergovernmental Flow of Funds." *National Tax Journal* 17: 75–85.

Sharkansky, Ira. 1967. "Economic and Political Correlates of State Government Expenditures: General Tendencies and Deviant Cases." *Midwest Journal of Political Science* 11: 173–92.

———. 1968. *Spending in the American States.* Chicago: Rand-McNally.

———. 1970. *The Routines of Politics.* New York: Van Nostrand Reinhold.

Sharkansky, Ira, and Richard Hofferbert. 1969. "Dimensions of State Politics, Economics, and Public Policy." *American Political Science Review* 63:867–79.

Slaughter, Sheila, and E.T. Silva. 1985. "Toward a Political Economy of Retrenchment." *Review of Higher Education* 8: 295–318.

Timm, Neil H. 1971. "A New Method of Measuring States' Higher Education Burden." *Journal of Higher Education* 42(1): 27–33.

Toregas, C. October 1988. "People, Services, and Technology." *State Government News* 8–9.

Turnbull, Augustus, and Patricia Irvin. 1984. "The Florida Appropriations Process—An Overview." In *State Budgeting in Florida,* edited by T. Foss and T. Sutberry. Tallahassee: Florida State Univ., Florida Center for Public Management.

U.S. Department of Education, National Center for Education Statistics. 1988. *Digest of Education Statistics, 1988.* Publication No. CS 88-600. Washington, D.C.: U.S. Government Printing Office. ED 295 344. 469 pp. MF–01; PC–19.

Volkwein, J. Fredericks. 1987. "State Regulation and Institutional Autonomy." Paper presented at an annual meeting of the Association for the Study of Higher Education, February, San Diego, California.

———. 1989. "Changes in Quality among Public Universities." *Journal of Higher Education* 60(2): 136–51.

Wallhaus, Robert A. 1982. "Process Issues in State-Level Program Reviews." In *Designing Academic Program Reviews,* edited by R. Wilson. New Directions for Higher Education No. 37. San Francisco: Jossey-Bass.

Wanat, J. 1974. "Bases of Budgetary Incrementalism." *American Political Science Review* 68: 1221–28.

Weld, E.A. 1972. "Expenditures for Public Institutions of Higher Education, 1969–70." *Journal of Higher Education* 43: 417–40.

Wildavsky, Aaron. 1984. *The Politics of the Budgetary Process.* 4th ed. Boston: Little, Brown & Co.

———. 1986. *Budgeting: A Comparative Theory of Budgetary Processes.* 2d rev. ed. New Brunswick, N.J.: Transaction Books.

Wirt, Frederick. 1976. "Education Politics and Policies." In *Politics in the American States: A Comparative Analysis,* edited by H. Jacob and K.N Vines. 3d ed. Boston: Little, Brown & Co.

Wirt, Frederick M., and Michael W. Kirst. 1972. *Political and Social Foundations of Education.* Berkeley, Cal.: McCutcheon.

Wirt, Frederick, Douglas Mitchell, and Catherine Marshall. 1988. "Culture and Education Policy: Analyzing Values in State Policy Systems." *Educational Evaluation and Policy Analysis* 10(4): 271–84.

Wittstruck, John R., and Stephen Bragg. 1988. "Focus on Price: Trends in Public Higher Education, Tuition, and State Support." Denver: State Higher Education Executive Officers. ED 299 879. 123 pp. MF–01; PC–05.

Zumeta, William. 1988a. "A Framework for Analysis of State Policy and Independent Higher Education." Denver: Education Commission of the States.

———. 1988b. "Survey of State Policies That May Affect Independent Higher Education." Denver: Education Commission of the States.

Zumeta, William, and Kenneth C. Green. 1987. "State Policies and Independent Higher Education: A Conceptual Framework and Some Empirical Findings, or Can the States Help the Private Sector Survive?" Paper presented at an annual meeting of the Association for the Study of Higher Education, February, San Diego, California. ED 281 454. 89 pp. MF–01; PC–04.

Zusman, Ami. 1986. "Legislature and University Conflict: The Case of California." *Review of Higher Education* 9(4): 397–418.

INDEX

A

Academic freedom, 29
Academic programs review, 56
Accountability
    fiduciary, 54
    mechanisms, 54
    procedural, 54
    substantive, 54
    systematic, 54
Affordability: higher education, 66
African-Americans
    higher education, 73
    recruitment, 74
Analysis: state higher education budgets, 79-90
Approaches to funding, 16
    evaluation, 19
    quality, 19
    technical expertise, 19
Appropriations and budgeting
    Illinois, 7
    Michigan, 7
Arizona: funds allocation, 51
Asians
    higher education, 73
    recruitment, 74
Auditing and budgets, 14

B

Budgets
    accountability, 53-54
    analysis and implications, 79
    approval, 14
    cost, productivity, and quality, 62
    outcomes, 8, 53
    research, 79
Budgetary needs
    economic variables, 9
    education, 8
    political variables, 8
Budgetary process, 42-44
    economic conditions, 45
    environmental context, 23, 45
Business partnerships: higher education, 71

C

California: community colleges, 16
Centers of excellence, 65

ASHE-ERIC HIGHER EDUCATION REPORTS

Since 1983, the Association for the Study of Higher Education (ASHE) and the Educational Resources Information Center (ERIC) Clearinghouse on Higher Education, a sponsored project of the School of Education and Human Development at The George Washington University, have cosponsored the *ASHE-ERIC Higher Education Report* series. The 1990 series is the nineteenth overall and the second to be published by the School of Education and Human Development at the George Washington University.

Each monograph is the definitive analysis of a tough higher education problem, based on thorough research of pertinent literature and insitutional experiences. Topics are identified by a national survey. Noted practitioners and scholars are then commissioned to write the reports, with experts providing critical reviews of each manuscript before publication.

Eight monographs (10 before 1985) in the ASHE-ERIC Higher Education Report series are published each year and are available on individual and subscription basis. Subscription to eight issues is $80.00 annually; $60 to members of AAHE, AIR, or AERA; and $50 to ASHE members. All foreign subscribers must include an additional $10 per series year for postage.

To order single copies of existing reports, use the order form on the last page of this book. Regular prices, and special rates available to members of AAHE, AIR, AERA and ASHE, are as follows:

Series	Regular	Members
1990	$17.00	$12.75
1988-89	15.00	11.25
1985-87	10.00	7.50
1983-84	7.50	6.00
before 1983	6.50	5.00

Price includes book rate postage within the U.S. For foreign orders, please add $1.00 per book. Fast United Parcel Service available within the contiguous U.S. at $2.50 for each order under $50.00, and calculated at 5% of invoice total for orders $50.00 or above.

All orders under $45.00 must be prepaid. Make check payable to ASHE-ERIC. For Visa or MasterCard, include card number, expiration date and signature. A bulk discount of 10% is available on orders of 15 or more books (not applicable on subscriptions).

Address order to
ASHE-ERIC Higher Education Reports
The George Washington University
1 Dupont Circle, Suite 630
Washington, DC 20036
Or phone (202) 296-2597
Write for a complete catalog of ASHE-ERIC Higher Education Reports.

1990 ASHE-ERIC Higher Education Reports

1. The Campus Green: Fund Raising in Higher Education
   Barbara E. Brittingham and Thomas R. Pezzullo

2. The Emeritus Professor: Old Rank - New Meaning
   James E. Mauch, Jack W. Birch, and Jack Matthews

3. "High Risk" Students in Higher Education: Future Trends
   Dionne J. Jones and Betty Collier Watson

1989 ASHE-ERIC Higher Education Reports

1. Making Sense of Administrative Leadership: The 'L' Word in Higher Education
   Estela M. Bensimon, Anna Neumann, and Robert Birnbaum

2. Affirmative Rhetoric, Negative Action: African-American and Hispanic Faculty at Predominantly White Universities
   Valora Washington and William Harvey

3. Postsecondary Developmental Programs: A Traditional Agenda with New Imperatives
   Louise M. Tomlinson

4. The Old College Try: Balancing Athletics and Academics in Higher Education
   John R. Thelin and Lawrence L. Wiseman

5. The Challenge of Diversity: Involvement or Alienation in the Academy?
   Daryl G. Smith

6. Student Goals for College and Courses: A Missing Link in Assessing and Improving Academic Achievement
   Joan S. Stark, Kathleen M. Shaw, and Malcolm A. Lowther

7. The Student as Commuter: Developing a Comprehensive Institutional Response
   Barbara Jacoby

8. Renewing Civic Capacity: Preparing College Students for Service and Citizenship
   Suzanne W. Morse

1988 ASHE-ERIC Higher Education Reports

1. The Invisible Tapestry: Culture in American Colleges and Universities
   George D. Kuh and Elizabeth J. Whitt

2. Critical Thinking: Theory, Research, Practice, and Possibilities
   Joanne Gainen Kurfiss

3. Developing Academic Programs: The Climate for Innovation
   Daniel T. Seymour

4. Peer Teaching: To Teach is To Learn Twice
   Neal A. Whitman

5. Higher Education and State Governments: Renewed Partnership,
   Cooperation, or Competition?
   Edward R. Hines

6. Entrepreneurship and Higher Education: Lessons for Colleges,
   Universities, and Industry
   James S. Fairweather

7. Planning for Microcomputers in Higher Education: Strategies
   for the Next Generation
   *Reynolds Ferrante, John Hayman, Mary Susan Carlson, and
   Harry Phillips*

8. The Challenge for Research in Higher Education: Harmonizing
   Excellence and Utility
   Alan W. Lindsay and Ruth T. Neumann

1987 ASHE-ERIC Higher Education Reports

1. Incentive Early Retirement Programs for Faculty: Innovative
   Responses to a Changing Environment
   Jay L. Chronister and Thomas R. Kepple, Jr.

2. Working Effectively with Trustees: Building Cooperative Campus
   Leadership
   Barbara E. Taylor

3. Formal Recognition of Employer-Sponsored Instruction: Conflict
   and Collegiality in Postsecondary Education
   Nancy S. Nash and Elizabeth M. Hawthorne

4. Learning Styles: Implications for Improving Educational Practices
   Charles S. Claxton and Patricia H. Murrell

5. Higher Education Leadership: Enhancing Skills through Professional Development Programs
   Sharon A. McDade

6. Higher Education and the Public Trust: Improving Stature in
   Colleges and Universities
   Richard L. Alfred and Julie Weissman

7. College Student Outcomes Assessment: A Talent Development
   Perspective
   Maryann Jacobi, Alexander Astin, and Frank Ayala, Jr.

8. Opportunity from Strength: Strategic Planning Clarified with
   Case Examples
   Robert G. Cope

1986 ASHE-ERIC Higher Education Reports

1. Post-tenure Faculty Evaluation: Threat or Opportunity?
   Christine M. Licata

2. Blue Ribbon Commissions and Higher Education: Changing Academe from the Outside
   Janet R. Johnson and Laurence R. Marcus

3. Responsive Professional Education: Balancing Outcomes and Opportunities
   Joan S. Stark, Malcolm A. Lowther, and Bonnie M.K. Hagerty

4. Increasing Students' Learning: A Faculty Guide to Reducing Stress among Students
   Neal A. Whitman, David C. Spendlove, and Claire H. Clark

5. Student Financial Aid and Women: Equity Dilemma?
   Mary Moran

6. The Master's Degree: Tradition, Diversity, Innovation
   Judith S. Glazer

7. The College, the Constitution, and the Consumer Student: Implications for Policy and Practice
   Robert M. Hendrickson and Annette Gibbs

8. Selecting College and University Personnel: The Quest and the Question
   Richard A. Kaplowitz

1985 ASHE-ERIC Higher Education Reports

1. Flexibility in Academic Staffing: Effective Policies and Practices
   Kenneth P. Mortimer, Marque Bagshaw, and Andrew T. Masland

2. Associations in Action: The Washington, D.C. Higher Education Community
   Harland G. Bloland

3. And on the Seventh Day: Faculty Consulting and Supplemental Income
   Carol M. Boyer and Darrell R. Lewis

4. Faculty Research Performance: Lessons from the Sciences and Social Sciences
   John W. Creswell

5. Academic Program Review: Institutional Approaches, Expectations, and Controversies
   Clifton F. Conrad and Richard F. Wilson

6. Students in Urban Settings: Achieving the Baccalaureate Degree
   Richard C. Richardson, Jr. and Louis W. Bender

7. Serving More Than Students: A Critical Need for College Student Personnel Services
   Peter H. Garland

8. Faculty Participation in Decision Making: Necessity or Luxury?
   Carol E. Floyd

1984 ASHE-ERIC Higher Education Reports

1. Adult Learning: State Policies and Institutional Practices
   K. Patricia Cross and Anne-Marie McCartan

2. Student Stress: Effects and Solutions
   Neal A. Whitman, David C. Spendlove, and Claire H. Clark

3. Part-time Faulty: Higher Education at a Crossroads
   Judith M. Gappa

4. Sex Discrimination Law in Higher Education: The Lessons of the Past Decade. ED 252 169.*
   J. Ralph Lindgren, Patti T. Ota, Perry A. Zirkel, and Nan Van Gieson

5. Faculty Freedoms and Institutional Accountability: Interactions and Conflicts
   Steven G. Olswang and Barbara A. Lee

6. The High Technology Connection: Academic/Industrial Cooperation for Economic Growth
   Lynn G. Johnson

7. Employee Educational Programs: Implications for Industry and Higher Education. ED 258 501.*
   Suzanne W. Morse

8. Academic Libraries: The Changing Knowledge Centers of Colleges and Universities
   Barbara B. Moran

9. Futures Research and the Strategic Planning Process: Implications for Higher Education
   James L. Morrison, William L. Renfro, and Wayne I. Boucher

10. Faculty Workload: Research, Theory, and Interpretation
    Harold E. Yuker

1983 ASHE-ERIC Higher Education Reports

1. The Path to Excellence: Quality Assurance in Higher Education
   Laurence R. Marcus, Anita O. Leone, and Edward D. Goldberg

2. Faculty Recruitment, Retention, and Fair Employment: Obligations and Opportunities
   John S. Waggaman

*Out-of-print. Available through EDRS. Call 1-800-227-ERIC.

ORDER FORM 90-4

Quantity **Amount**

_____ Please send a complete set of the 1989 *ASHE-ERIC Higher Education Reports* at $80.00, 33% off the cover price. _____

_____ Please begin my subscription to the 1990 *ASHE-ERIC Higher Education Reports* at $80.00, 41% off the cover price, starting with Report 1, 1990 _____

_____ Outside the U.S., add $10 per series for postage _____

Individual reports are avilable at the following prices:

1990 and forward, $17.00	1983 and 1984, $7.50
1988 and 1989, $15.00	1982 and back, $6.50
1985 to 1987, $10.00	

Book rate postage within the U.S. is included. Outside U.S., please add $1 per book for postage. Fast U.P.S. shipping is available within the contiguous U.S. at $2.50 for each order under $50.00, and calculated at 5% of invoice total for orders $50.00 or above. All orders under $45 must be prepaid.

PLEASE SEND ME THE FOLLOWING REPORTS:

Quantity	Report No.	Year	Title	Amount
			Subtotal:	
			Foreign or UPS:	
			Total Due:	

Please check one of the following:

☐ Check enclosed, payable to GWU-ERIC.
☐ Purchase order attached ($45.00 minimum).
☐ Charge my credit card indicated below:
    ☐ Visa   ☐ MasterCard

Expiration Date _____

Name _____

Title _____

Institution _____

Address _____

City _____ State _____ Zip _____

Phone _____

Signature _____ Date _____

SEND ALL ORDERS TO:
ASHE-ERIC Higher Education Reports
The George Washington University
One Dupont Circle, Suite 630
Washington, DC 20036-1183
Phone: (202) 296-2597